Managing to Succeed

Managing to Succeed

True to Our Roots
Fermenting a Business Revolution

Paul Dolan

with

Thom Elkjer

Viva Books

New Delhi | Mumbai | Chennai | Kolkata | Bengaluru | Hyderabad | Kochi | Guwahati

Indian Edition 2011

VIVA BOOKS PRIVATE LIMITED

- 4737/23 Ansari Road, Daryaganj, New Delhi 110 002
  E-mail: vivadelhi@vivagroupindia.net, Tel. 42242200
- 76, Service Industries, Shirvane, Sector 1, Nerul, Navi Mumbai 400 706
  E-mail: vivamumbai@vivagroupindia.net, Tel. 27721273, 27721274
- Jamals Fazal Chambers, 26 Greams Road, Chennai 600 006
  E-mail: vivachennai@vivagroupindia.net, Tel. 28290304, 28294241
- B-103, Jindal Towers, 21/1A/3 Darga Road, Kolkata 700 017
  E-mail: vivakolkata@vivagroupindia.net, Tel. 22836381, 22816713
- 7, Sovereign Park Apartments, 56-58, K. R. Road, Basavanagudi, Bengaluru 560 004
  E-mail: vivabangalore@vivagroupindia.net, Tel. 26607409, 26607410
- 101-102 Mughal Marc Apartments, 3-4-637 to 641, Narayanguda, Hyderabad 500 029
  E-mail: vivahyderabad@vivagroupindia.net, Tel. 27564481, 27564482
- First Floor, Beevi Towers, SRM Road, Kaloor, Kochi 682 018, Kerala
  E-mail: vivakochi@vivagroupindia.net, Tel: 0484-2403055, 2403056
- 232, GNB Road, Beside UCO Bank, Silpukhuri, Guwahati 781 003
  E-mail: vivaguwahati@vivagroupindia.net, Tel: 0361-2666386

www.vivagroupindia.com

Published by arrangement with
Bloomberg Press
100 Business Park Drive
PO Box No. 888, Princeton
NJ 08542-0888, USA

ISBN : 978-81-309-1704-7

Published by Vinod Vasishtha for Viva Books Private Limited, 4737/23, Ansari Road, Daryaganj, New Delhi-110 002. Printed and bound by Anand Sons, Delhi.

This book is dedicated to everyone at Fetzer Vineyards for their creative, can-do approach to business.

CONTENTS

ACKNOWLEDGMENTS

Special thanks to my wife Diana for her support, interest, and encouragement throughout this project; to my daughter Sassicaia for her patience and understanding (especially on weekends); and to my brother Peter for his ongoing friendship and challenging me to be the best I can be. Much appreciation also goes to Pat Voss, Guy Goodacre, Jill Jepson, and Carol Crosby, my colleagues at Fetzer Vineyards who contributed ideas, examples, and organization throughout the project; to my friend Neal Rogin, who helped me identify and articulate the principles underlying Fetzer's success; and to Paul Hawken, who transformed my understanding of what a business could be. *PAUL DOLAN*

Thanks to Paul Dolan for creating the space for me to contribute, to Kimberly Charles for making the connection and Arthur Klebanoff for cementing it, and to my wife Antoinette for her unconditional support. *THOM ELKJER*

PREFACE

This is a book we had to write.

After twenty-five years at Fetzer Vineyards, including more than a decade as the company's president and visionary leader on the road to sustainability, Paul Dolan had not only generated a set of guiding leadership principles and collected the stories to illustrate them, he had also seen how Fetzer's success was influencing a profound change of attitude in the wine business. The more he looked beyond his own industry, the more powerfully he felt the need to serve the world by sharing his hard-won insights and examples with everyone, in every industry, who could possibly benefit from them.

I had been writing articles about the sustainability sea change in the wine business, with the professed aim of accelerating it. When Paul invited me to talk about collaborating on a book, it was clear that he had the goods: passion, experience, and inspired determination to create a more sustainable world. As we talked on an autumn morning in a small café on the Mendocino Coast, I felt my own commitment to the earth and its inhabitants growing stronger by the minute. Working with Paul since that time has deepened my understanding of what he has accomplished—and how much we all can learn from it.

We're both pleased to honor the memory of Barney Fetzer, who before his untimely death in 1981 wrote a brief memoir about finding a run-down ranch in northern California and planting the seeds that years later became Fetzer Vineyards. An excerpt of that memoir follows as a testament to pioneering spirits everywhere.

THOM ELKJER

FOREWORD

I found it on a Sunday afternoon in October, 1958. An abandoned ranch, the old Smith place, surrounded by poorly cared for vineyards in a valley all by itself—nine miles from the Mendocino County Courthouse, yet so remote that it seemed a guarantee of a peace and emotional security I had long sought.

The old house was a tall, two-story affair, rambling and rickety. Bats and owls nested in the tall chimney, and gardens with their rampant lilacs and roses were full. Coveys of valley quail fed on the crimson pyracantha bushes. People said the house was hopeless, absolutely unsafe, and uninhabitable. Others told me the vineyards were not worth another pruning or cultivation—phylloxera had taken its toll. Poison oak crowded around every vine, live and pin oak grew fifteen feet high in the vineyard rows.

I was drawn to the place like a magnet. I pondered. I dreamed. I checked the balances in the savings and checking accounts. I checked the cash balances in my life insurance policies again and again. I discussed. I gathered facts. Taxes. Machinery. The future of wine grapes. We inspected the underpinnings of the house, tore boards off and looked for termites, jumped on the floors, drew sketches, imagined what it would look like after knocking walls out, estimated replumbing and rewiring.

Every spare moment I had was spent going over all 720 acres of this property. Corners were found. Old timers were talked to, their remarks were weighed and then, usually discarded. One Saturday I walked to the westernmost line, one mile above the old house, then headed north down the mountain to Seward Creek and down past huge pools of cold mountain spring water flashing with wily trout. Deer thrashed out of the alder and pepperwood groves ahead of me, then turned halfway up steep glades to watch me. It was here—along the creek, in the ageless silence of an autumn afternoon—that I made up my mind to buy the ranch and spend the rest of my life.

In January of 1959, on New Year's Day, I started trucking tools and lumber to the old house. The ranch is two miles long—a long strip up the valley—and the main ranchstead is in the center. Each time I passed the last gatepost, a curtain of peace seemed to drop around everything. I started building an old bedroom wing into a new kitchen, working along with John, my eldest son, many times until midnight.

Then we drove the 14 cold or rain-swept miles back east of the river to our home in town. My dreams kept expanding, but were intermittently disrupted with financial worries and imagined trouble. All our money was in this endeavor, and it looked insurmountable. I recalled the many remarks of the people I had talked with prior to my decision. One haunted me. The Smiths never had water. They piped it out of the creek in the summer. Water was essential. It worried me. When I turned the faucets on in the old house, there was a gurgle, then a slow tepid flow of rusty, clay-silted water from the spigots. The old gravity system on the mountain above the house was inadequate. It would not do. A gasoline pump in the creek 100 yards below had to be started each morning and night. Many times it would not start.

So I decided to drill a well. I studied witching. Talked financing. Talked to old timers again. They showed me the multitude of holes—all dry—up every canyon, even dry holes right along the creek, that beautiful creek where water abounded throughout the year.

January and February passed. A family of Mexicans who lived in a small cabin on the lower part of the ranch were pruning 27,000 grapevines, each carefully cut back to two buds. I leased the pear orchard. The hillsides and meadows were rampant with heavy grass. We bought 50 old ewes, wild-eyed and skinny, and turned them loose. I bought two white-faced cows and put them in the 300-acre south pasture. Bills mounted. Spring came. There was not time for all the work, and soon it would be time to start the long job of cultivating vineyards.

I found myself gradually being entirely possessed with the project: sleeping alone in the house nights, bringing the three boys with me on week-ends, cooking our meals over a Coleman stove in the empty house, waking up at night to hear the rats tearing around the attics above.

The well drillers moved in; they went 25 feet and hit a tremendous stream, went another 40 feet for added storage, and pulled the rig out. We have an abundance of water! The house progressed. A large fireplace was built in the kitchen. The plumbing was the toughest, and I hated the smell of pipe compound and the patience and time it took to place the pipes. Pruning of the vineyards was completed. We took the tractors into the vineyards—a wobbly old crawler and a temperamental Fordson. Cultivating fascinated me: the smell of the rich, fresh-turned bottom ground, the churning up of the heavy cover crop, the early morning stillness broken only by the squeak of the disk and the noise of the tractor. Here was a place where a man could let his thoughts wander and expand.

So we were pulled even farther into this way of living, and when Kathleen, my wife, saw that it was no longer a passing whim, she seriously prepared to move to the ranch—however, very reluctantly, as she was afraid, most unhappy with the old house, expecting her eighth child soon, and downright baffled by this complete change in family life.

Then came mid-April and the apprehension and fear of frost on the tender shoots of the vines. And it came. Late in April the frost whitened the barn roof and covered the vineyards. And then the sun came out, the leaves had curled black and shriveled, and the people who farm the vineyards took the ravages in silence, many of them not going into the fields to even look. People said we were wiped out, that it was a terrible loss. Then the hillsides sported their delicate colors—wildflowers everywhere. The buckeye leafed. The black oak took on color. Lambs came and frolicked on the mountain meadows. The quail sang their mating songs everywhere. The grapes came back with secondary budding. Mornings our valley rang with merriment, and the tractors went tearing through the vineyards—the second time around.

Farming—like no other way of life—teaches man's great dependency on the Supreme Being: the necessity of patience, philosophical attitudes, hope. Moments of despair, yes, but each one countered with a moment of triumph.

BERNARD ("BARNEY") FETZER
1920–1981

TRUE TO OUR ROOTS

INTRODUCTION

SUSTAINABILITY: FETZER'S BUSINESS REVOLUTION

On a crisp September morning in 1987, I was walking through a block of Sauvignon Blanc vines at Fetzer Vineyards. I was the head winemaker, and this early stroll through the vineyards was one of my favorite rituals.

The grape harvest was just getting under way, and soon I would be inside the cellar, managing a big crew amidst the hustle and bustle of what California winemakers call "crush." That's the hectic period in early autumn when grapes are picked and pressed, and their juice flows into tanks to begin fermenting into wine. But for now I was where I loved to be, alone with nature in the still of the dawn, using all my senses to smell the soil, inspect the ripening bunches, and taste the grapes.

Sauvignon Blanc is a fruity white wine, crisp and refreshing. It delivers these qualities in abundance when it's grown in Mendocino County, where warm days are separated by cool nights. It was up to me to decide when these grapes would be picked—a real moment of truth in the wine business. Pick too early or too late, and you miss the time when the fruit is precisely ripe enough and full of flavor, perfectly ready to become the best wine you will ever make.

I had been making wine professionally for ten years, so biting into a wine grape gave me a lot of information. I first tasted for the slightly bitter acids in the skin. These components would give the wine its crisp, mouthwatering quality. Then I tasted for the natural sugars in the juice, which would give the wine its flavors, aromas, and body. In the rows where I was tasting, the grapes were infused with lush, creamy flavors of ripe figs and melon, perfect for Sauvignon Blanc. The vines had produced a sweetness and balance, in harmony with the sun, soil, and clean air surrounding them.

These grapes were ready to pick, and my excitement started to build. I began thinking of how I would manage the grapes in the winery. I would not have to do too much, because nature had already done so well. My job would be largely to let the wine reveal itself.

When I moved to the next block, just fifteen short feet away, my excitement quickly subsided. These Sauvignon Blanc grapes tasted bland. Every grape seemed less flavorful, less expressive. My euphoria faded. Before I had time to figure out this mystery, the sun crested the eastern hills and fully loaded grape trucks started rumbling up the driveway. Crush was on.

I hustled back to the winery and forgot about my experience in the vineyard until hours later. At the end of that day, as I planned the next day's picking schedule, my mind wandered back to the two Sauvignon Blanc blocks that had tasted so different. They were grown in the same microclimate, irrigated the same way, and the vines were the same age. What explained the difference in taste?

Slowly it dawned on me. The first block of vines was part of an experiment we had begun the year before, farming some of our vineyards organically. The second block was still being farmed the conventional way. That meant we applied pesticides, herbicides, and fungicides throughout the growing season. Then we replenished what we'd stripped from the soil by adding back synthetic chemical fertilizers. This was the way everyone did it. It was the approach I learned when I studied enology, and it was the gospel our local agricultural extension experts preached. It was standard operating procedure.

I didn't know it then, but my entire way of thinking about grape growing was about to change, with huge ramifications for me personally and for Fetzer. Before that moment, I had only read about the impact of pesticides on the environment. I hadn't ever experienced the effect they could have on flavor. Now, I was tasting it firsthand. My mind raced as I realized that the synthetic chemicals had removed all the natural microbial richness from the vineyard earth—they had stripped the life from the soil. Just one year without chemicals had allowed the other block of vines to bounce back and produce fresher, brighter flavors.

The implications staggered me. I am a fourth-generation winemaker. My great-grandfather Pietro Carlo Rossi worked at Italian Swiss Colony in Asti, California, for most of his adult life. He lived and breathed winemaking, and in 1904 he built a large home near the winery. My grandfather Edmund grew up there and eventually became a winemaker for Italian Swiss Colony, too. When my siblings and I were born, we used to spend a month each summer at the house in Asti, having the run of the winery and eating cookies out of small wine barrels in the tasting room. A huge board there had medals pinned to it—awards for my great-grandfather's, grandfather's, and uncle's wines. I saw them as our family medals. We still have the family house and now it is my children and grandchildren who play there with their cousins all summer. So for over 100 years, my family has had roots up and down the Russian River, the long, vital watercourse that arises in Mendocino County and flows south through Sonoma County to the Pacific Ocean. The river that waters our gardens and fills our wells here literally flows through my veins, just as Mendocino's cool, crisp air filled my lungs that harvest morning. I knew I was part of the fabric of this place. It was my land, my heritage, the home of my children—and my winery was poisoning it.

If that wasn't bad enough, I could see that continued use of chemicals at nearly every step of the grape-growing process would diminish the quality of future vintages, most certainly affecting the long-term market position of the winery. If I could taste this drastic a difference in the grapes already, what would another few decades of this approach mean to the flavor of our wines? These were chilling realizations for a young, ambitious winemaker. It was very clear to me that Fetzer Vineyards and, for that matter, all other wineries were risking not only their own economic futures but the long-term viability of all farming. It was an inherently unsustainable position. The wine industry could not continue with standard operating procedure, and neither could I.

A NEW POSSIBILITY FOR BUSINESS

IF YOU HAVE HAD a life-changing experience like mine, you know how it feels. One moment your world looks a certain way, and the next, it looks different. Things that you could ignore, or set aside, or avoid, become a permanent part of your awareness. Issues in the world that used to be outside of your purview are now living inside of you. They become emotional and physical, not just intellectual. Similar awareness might have to do with corruption on Wall Street, or destruction of the environment, or a desperate need for human rights. It may have to do with the way your own company operates. Whatever it is, it changes you. Something that's not right with the world is now not right for you.

Suddenly, you're wondering what you can do about it. You realize you must act.

I believe we are all feeling this at some level. It doesn't matter what our political orientation is. It doesn't matter how much money we make. It doesn't matter where we live. Global warming affects us all, regardless of socioeconomic position. America's crash in investor confidence took its toll on everyone's finances. The Chernobyl disaster was dramatic proof that a few small slip-ups by inadequately trained workers could wipe out everything for miles around and send nuclear fallout drifting across a dozen countries. Scientists talk about climate change, droughts, and floods not as isolated events, but as evidence that Earth is one biosphere, without barriers. Whatever we do on this planet stays on this planet and affects all its inhabitants. Hunger and disease epidemics and massacres half a world away may not hurt anyone we know personally, but we know in our hearts that something should be done. We know the world needs to change, because the path we're on doesn't look good.

This book is about how I rediscovered my roots and decided to change paths. It is a book about a new possibility for business, one that will require nothing less than a revolution within organizations, and among managers and workers of all stripes. Fortunately, no one has to be overthrown in this revolution; we just need to replace standard operating procedure with something more sustainable. Everyone can participate in this process, and everyone can benefit. In fact, I believe many people already see this revolution coming, and are wondering how and where and when it will affect them.

The premise of this book is this: We can lead the revolution ourselves without waiting for it to hit. We can bring it on, and take it where we want to go. We simply have to reconnect with what's important and practice the principles of sustainable leadership that arise from that experience. I believe it's time for business, one of the most powerful forces on Earth, to become a positive force for change. We already know that we can create tremendous wealth and technological progress. The new possibility for those of us in business is to preserve that progress and wealth for the generations to come.

When I realized that my own company was not operating in a sustainable way, that an entire industry was doing things that were detrimental to its own economic and environmental health, I had to ask why. It appeared to stay this way because people simply didn't question it. Wine is full of wonder, but no one was taking the time to wonder about the business of wine. I started to read books about the environment and ecology. I visited with older farmers who had managed their vineyards and orchards without the kind of chemicals we have today. I challenged my former professors about what they had taught me. I questioned everything.

I also began to look more closely around me. I saw that the rugged, rural beauty of Mendocino didn't insulate us from troubling trends taking place around the world. Big global companies were using places such as Bangkok, Singapore, and Shanghai for cheap production locations, causing these cities to go through massive changes. Sweatshops and assembly facilities sprang up almost overnight. Living wages and working conditions diverged even further between the first world and the developing world. This same dramatic gap in income and economic participation swept through the wine industry, too. As the number of wineries and vineyard acres grew rapidly, so did the number of pickers and cellar workers.

Yet many wineries paid them minimum wage for backbreaking work, while providing no health benefits, housing, or training support that might help them in a continuing way. The value of grapes soared even as the needs of the workers were ignored. Wealthy people from all walks of life were cruising into the wine country and building immense villas. They didn't think twice about ripping out trees, bulldozing hillsides for questionable vineyards, and hiring staffs of servants. All these actions emphasized further that the wine industry was becoming two worlds that existed side by side, but unequally.

The more aware I became, the more I realized I could not ignore it any longer. Living in ignorance was bad enough. Living in deliberate denial was unacceptable. I loved making wine, but I didn't see how I would make my mark on society by doing that. It seemed that I had to leave the business world to make a difference, for myself and for others. Many people do follow this route when they discover things they cannot ignore. They leave jobs to become teachers, or join groups such as Doctors Without Borders, or become social workers. Business is not the usual place for someone who wants to change the world.

I was not unaware that I was leading what many would consider a privileged life. I lived in one of the most beautiful places on Earth, surrounded by lush vineyards, orchards of fruit and nut trees, towering redwood trees and majestic oaks. I worked for a highly respected wine family, with deep roots in the community. My own family was blessed with three wonderful children and a wife I loved and admired. I was indeed fortunate, and I loved my life. But something was still missing. The question lodged in my mind and would not let me go: How could I make a bigger difference? Where could I find a new possibility for my life, for my future, for my world?

BECOMING AN EXAMPLE

I WAS FORTUNATE, because fate intervened and offered me a unique chance right inside my own business. Before I could leave Fetzer Vineyards and go make my mark in some other field, Brown-Forman Corporation bought the company and appointed me president of the winery in 1992. You might not immediately recognize the Brown-Forman name, but if you have ever used Hartmann luggage or Lenox china, or enjoyed a glass of Jack Daniels Tennessee whiskey, Southern Comfort, Finlandia vodka, or wines from Bolla, Korbel, or Sonoma-Cutrer, then you have patronized one of Brown-Forman's many brands. Like Fetzer, Brown-Forman is a company with deep family roots.

When I was given the responsibility of running Fetzer, everything crystallized for me. Here was an opportunity to make a difference as a winemaker, and I was determined to take advantage of it. I didn't have a master plan or anything like it, just one heck of an opportunity. I stepped through the opening and never looked back. I moved immediately to steer the company into a new course, one that would be described today as "sustainable."

The employees of the company rallied to this new possibility with inspiring passion and creativity. Together we learned that our business is part of the larger world, just as all of us are part of it as individuals. If we personally desire to make a difference in the larger system, then our companies can, too.

That simple affirmation has changed the context for everything we do at Fetzer. The people of Fetzer have truly become the soul of the business—willing to put their hearts into it and live what they know. The more they achieve, the more they know, and that knowledge spurs them to achieve even more. Despite a mood of growing complexity and volatility, we are more confident than ever that we have the ability to create our own future.

As the leader of the company during the past ten years, I have learned as much as I have led. Watching the employees of Fetzer rise to this new possibility in their business, I have been acutely aware that everyone wants their lives to matter. We know there is only limited satisfaction in going through the motions of any given day. We know we want to enhance the quality of life for those around us. We want the world to have a future we can live in, and live with.

If you're not that familiar with Fetzer Vineyards, you might think that all this talk about changing the world is easy for the head of a little boutique winery in northern California. You might think that before I tell you about a new possibility for business, I should try running an industry-leading corporation that's slugging it out in a global marketplace, fending off low-cost imports, managing multiple production facilities, leading employees with diverse cultural backgrounds, adapting to constantly shifting regulations, and responding to health, safety, and employment laws that are tightening all the time.

Actually, that is a pretty good summary of what it's like to run Fetzer Vineyards.

Fetzer is the largest California brand in the United States for premium wines in the $7 to $10 range, and we make nearly four million cases of wine each year. We compete head-to-head with all the biggest California wineries you can name, including Gallo, Mondavi, and Kendall-Jackson—and also with the other 1,000-plus wineries in the state. Many of our competitors are owned not by farmers concerned about the long-term health of the vineyard, or by vintners seeking a fair return on investment to assure the health of their business, but by wealthy hobbyists whose decision making defies the principles of economics and ecology.

And California is only one piece of the equation. We also compete with wineries from across the United States and all over the world. There are approximately 6,500 wine brands sold in the United States, according to data compiled by a leading industry research firm, Gomberg, Frederikson & Associates. Those 6,500 brands are owned by thousands of wineries in this country and abroad, including multinational beverage giants you may know through the financial pages, such as Constellation, Diageo, Southcorp, and Allied Domecq, among others. The companies based overseas all want to sell in the United States. Some countries, notably Australia, have focused their entire industry on exporting, with the United States as a priority target market.

In short, the wine business is one of the most competitive global industries on Earth. There is terrific jockeying for our shelf space in stores, our spots on restaurant wine lists, our time with wholesalers, retailers, and wine critics, and our space at public events. Still, we're holding our own and growing steadily. In 2002, Fetzer was one of the ten best-selling brands in the United States, as measured by sales for all varietal wines at all price points. Some would say we rank even higher in terms of quality. *Wine & Spirits* magazine covers the entire range of wineries, from the smallest to the largest, and rates all products with equal professional rigor. They named Fetzer Vineyards "Winery of the Year" in its price and volume category not once but seven times in the 1990s. In 1998 and 2002, Fetzer wines won more medals at the California State Fair than any other winery, based on blind tastings by professional judges.

Our legal and regulatory environment also imposes some serious challenges. In the United States, alcoholic beverages are sold through a three-tier distribution system that is mandated by federal law. This means wineries cannot sell directly to the retailers and restaurants that sell wine to the public. We must go through wholesalers—and still reach out to the restaurants, retailers, and consumers directly to maintain demand for our products.

So we must be experts at packaging, branding, advertising and marketing, and distribution. We're based in agriculture, with all its issues of land use, water rights, climate change, and seasonal unpredictability. Technology is advancing as fast in the wine business as everywhere else, so we're constantly facing new investment decisions we've never had to make before, often involving multimillion-dollar rolls of the dice.

Against this background, Fetzer Vineyards' increased earnings an average of 15 percent a year through the 1990s, while keeping its environmental and social responsibilities as top priorities. Our experience proves that operating on a more sustainable basis is not an economic liability. If anything, we see sustainability as an economic asset and a competitive advantage.

Today, we farm all the vineyards we own organically, and we're the largest California grower of organic wine grapes as certified by California Certified Organic Farmers (CCOF). We're helping dozens more independent growers convert to organic farming as well, and providing an example that is inspiring the whole California wine industry to rethink its agricultural practices.

There are plenty of small, boutique wineries that are taking good care of their land, but by and large the bigger farmers are a traditionally conservative bunch, and they are prone to think that sustainability is for someone else. As long as most people believe that, there's no pressure to rethink what they are doing. Fetzer is helping to change this perception because of its size. "It's great to see more small, premium-priced wineries growing organically, but that's not what's going to change the industry," says Ehren Jordan, the winemaker at Turley Wine Cellars in Napa Valley. Like Fetzer, Turley farms its own acreage organically, and is working to convert all its outside growers to organic farming. The difference is, Turley makes only 10,000 to 12,000 cases of wine annually, and sells it for up to $75 a bottle. "Our example is not going to convert the big farmers," Ehren continues. "What's going to make people give up their excuses for using pesticides is when someone is growing organically and selling a million cases at six bucks a bottle."

Fetzer is nearly there now, and our industry is paying attention.

IMPORTANT RAMIFICATIONS

THINKING ABOUT our business in a sustainable way has had other important ramifications. In the past 10 years, we have reduced the amount of waste we haul to landfills by 93 percent—while increasing our production volume by 100 percent. We became the first winery in the United States to create a fully recyclable aluminum capsule for our bottles, which we have used since 1992. We purchase renewable energy for all winery and visitor center operations. We filter our own wastewater naturally, in a system we built at the winery, and we're phasing in bio-diesel to replace petroleum-based fuel in our winery vehicles and at our trucking company.

In 2002, Fetzer earned the Stratospheric Ozone Protection award from the United States Environmental Protection Agency, which earlier had given us a "Climate Wise" Partnership Award. The State of California has included Fetzer in its Waste Reduction Awards Program (WRAP) for the past seven years. In 1999, *Business Ethics* magazine awarded Fetzer its "Award for Environmental Excellence." In 2001, in the tenth anniversary issue of *The Green Business Letter*, author and environmentalist Joel Makower ranked Fetzer third in his list of companies worldwide that are most honored for being "environmentally progressive."

At Fetzer, we're just as determined to enrich social equity as we are to preserve the environment, and there are few organizations giving out prizes for that. We do it because it comes naturally out of the culture we've created. Fetzer's benefits programs, our community outreach programs, and our relationship with local businesses have been transformed over the past ten years, and we're continually discovering new ways to enhance them all. We support a wide range of community events and services that improve the places where our employees live. Our workforce is becoming more bilingual by the day, so we can better bridge the cultural gap between workers from different backgrounds. Many of our employees serve on industry and organization boards and help lead community nonprofits. Although we have grown rapidly and added new challenges for every worker in every department in the company for years now, our annual turnover rate is around 1 percent—far below the norm for the wine business, or any business.

When we changed course in 1992, we didn't even know what results we should be aiming for. There were almost no models, and we were located way out in the country, far from most other large businesses. So we relied on three things to move us forward. First was a willingness to admit we didn't know how to run a sustainable business. We had to discover how to do that, through a process of constant exploration. Second, we had to assume that everyone in the company had more to offer than just their job description, and that if we fully respected and acknowledged the human spirit in everyone, they would deliver the ideas and energy we needed. Third, we never stopped talking about what we were up to. Even now, we keep the conversation going nonstop, at every level of the business, so that no one ever wonders what our purpose is or where we are going.

In recent years, I have begun to explore how to share what we learned at Fetzer, so that I could offer it to other businesses and other leaders. I noticed certain attributes of the company that stood out. Somehow our process of exploration, our respect for each other, and our constant conversation about sustainability revealed some enduring truths about ourselves, our company, and a new possibility for business.

CHANGING THE PREMISE OF BUSINESS

HOW ARE WE DIFFERENT? The fundamental premise of business has long been that the genius of pure self-interest combined with the motivation of competition will produce wealth for the many, which benefits society as a whole. Those benefits to society, however, are secondary. The primary goal is producing returns for shareholders, which is what people mean when they say that "the business of business is business."

The assumption hidden in this argument is that the profits that businesses produce justify whatever resources must be taken from the earth and whatever business practices it takes to turn those resources into products. Now we see that this belief is flawed.

Natural resources are not unlimited, and human beings are not expendable. Profits don't justify strip-mining the wilderness or locking people to sewing machines in sweatshops. The true cost of a gallon of gas is not the price you pay at the pump. The true cost has to be measured in broader terms, to include what it costs the earth when oil is extracted and the cost when some of its byproducts return to the atmosphere, affecting humanity as a whole through global warming.

I recently read Jim Collins's powerful book, *Good to Great* (HarperCollins, 2001). He suggests that there may be many ways to compare and evaluate companies. But there is only one sure-fire measure that's worked to compare businesses across industries, and across time, in order to determine if they have moved from merely good to undeniably great—the change in the price of their stock. He does acknowledge that there are other measures of business impact, such as environmental responsibility and social equity. He even agrees these factors are important. But he still argues that there is simply no uniform measurement available for comparison except the change in stock price over time. His analysis is a good reflection of how the world views business today.

Stock price may indeed be a useful measure for investors to keep track of what happens to their money, but that is not all that business creates, and it's certainly not all that can be measured. The world is not crying out for ever-increasing stock prices. The world is crying out for companies to realize they can make an even bigger contribution, moving from merely good to undeniably great by making the world a better place.

When the idea of corporations was being developed two centuries ago, the world's resources appeared unlimited. Whole continents were still up for grabs. Making money by taking resources from other places and adding value seemed to have no downside. Enslaving or destroying other cultures presented no danger to the shareholders at home. Just being able to build factories and engines was a wonderful thing in the nineteenth century. No one knew anything about pollution. There was so much to take, it seemed all right if a company's profits were the beginning and end of its responsibility. Everyone was better off all the time, at least in the industrialized world, and the developing world was not an issue environmentally or socially.

Today it's different. The corporation remains a great vehicle for generating wealth and spreading it around. It's the world that has changed. Nonrenewable resources are running out. Economic imbalances are becoming social, political, and even military threats to world order. Nothing takes place in isolation, especially not in a world with a twenty-four-hour news cycle. We now see that there are more stakeholders in a business than its owners, and the interests of the various stakeholders can diverge sharply.

SUSTAINABLE SUCCESS

THE NEW POSSIBILITY for business is to see this as a positive, not negative. Business has resources, organization, an orientation toward goals and results—everything we need to help make the world a better place. It may be that business is now the most powerful institution on Earth, the one institution capable of steering humanity onto profitable pathways that don't lead to humanity's demise. For business to play that role, we need to shift our awareness and act from a new premise: that the business of business is sustaining its long-term success.

So what does sustainable success look like?

For me, a successful sustainable business is one that provides steady shareholder returns while improving the quality of life of its workers, the communities it calls home, and the environment it touches. Its strategic perspective reaches out beyond the next four quarters, beyond the next five years, to consider what's ahead for the next generation. It is prosperous without being wasteful. It grows without mortgaging its future. It shares its discoveries without giving up its leadership. A successful business lives by its principles, and each new challenge is an opportunity to express those principles more fully, not abandon them conveniently.

Today I can understand what sets Fetzer's way of working apart from most other businesses. Here are the distinguishing features, which I believe any organization can emulate.

Your Business Is Part of a Much Larger System

At Fetzer, we proceed from the principle that we are part of a huge, interconnected web of relationships. None of us is alone. Every one of us, all our communities, and all our businesses share one planet and one future. All our actions, and their consequences, remain inside this larger system, reverberating and creating new consequences—for better or worse.

The Culture of Your Business Is Determined by the Context You Create for It

Everything in life gets its meaning from its context. We used to think that the larger system we live in, planet Earth, offered us an unlimited natural wealth. Now we see diminishing resources and accelerating species extinction. One of the first things we did at Fetzer Vineyards was to consciously set a context that inspired people to respond, in a personal way, to the challenge of building a sustainable business. With the right culture, sustainability shifted from a concept to concerted action; it was woven into the fabric of the company, not dictated from above.

The Soul of a Business Is Found in the Hearts of Its People

One of the turning points for us was when people began shifting from accountability to responsibility—from delivering the predefined results in their job descriptions to taking up the larger challenge of transforming the business. Leaders can inspire that shift by seeing people as the source of sustainability, not a resource for it, and by constantly acknowledging their contributions.

True Power Is Living What You Know

Once we saw our business within a larger system, once we had a context for making a difference, and once we were encouraged to make that difference in our jobs, everyone at Fetzer found a new source of personal and organization power. The source of that power was integrity. At Fetzer, living what we knew about the land, our people, and our community generated a wealth of new understanding—a virtuous cycle of knowledge and empowerment. Now that we see our examples can inspire and enable others, we share whatever we can.

You Can't Predict the Future, but You Can Create It

Many companies are oriented toward short-term goals rather than a larger purpose. Sustainability requires that we orient ourselves toward the larger purpose, because this orientation will naturally organize the process for achieving it. At Fetzer, we create the future by visualizing the future and then painting a vivid picture of new possibilities and managing our business from that perspective.

There Is a Way to Make an Idea's Time Come

Many businesses have taken positions on the environment, or social issues. At Fetzer, we have found that to really make an idea's time come, we have to take more than a position. We have to take a stand. Positions are relative and reactive, stands are absolute and proactive. Now that our business has taken a stand for sustainability, everyone in the company is personally engaged, responsible for its realization, and open to whatever path that completion might take. Taking a stand publicly produced immediate results in the wine industry, by expanding people's understanding of what's possible for them, their companies, and their world.

I'LL BE EXPLORING each of these distinguishing features of sustainable business in its own chapter. Some readers might find one or more principles that they can begin applying and incorporating into their business right away. Others might take more time to think and talk about. The most important thing is to explore them for yourself and discover how they can serve you in the cause of sustainable business.

EXPLORATION AND DISCOVERY

EXPOSING YOUR TASTE BUDS to a multitude of wines is an essential part of any winemaker's education. I did a little of this as a kid, with the professional winemakers in my family, but it wasn't until I studied winemaking at California State University in Fresno that I really got serious. I was particularly excited to be invited to join a wine-tasting group organized by Ken Brown (who later launched his own California winery, called Byron). This was both an honor and a challenge for a budding winemaker, and I prepared excitedly for my first tasting with the group. The wine category was California Chardonnay—not nearly as common then as it is today—and I did my research. I bought the appropriate wines ahead of time, I tasted them, and I was sure I could identify their distinguishing features. I was feeling pretty confident when the tasting got under way.

But when we sat down, my confidence deserted me. There were ten glasses of Chardonnay, and they all smelled the same. I was getting the same impression, the same characteristics from every glass. I tasted through the wines again, more quickly, with a growing sense of panic. We were supposed to put the ten wines in order of preference, but how could I do that when I could not detect any difference among them at all?

I survived that tasting, but I never forget that learning about wine is a constant process of discovery. It's the same with building a sustainable business. No amount of forethought totally prepares you for something you've never done before. There are very few signposts along the way, and it's not even clear where we should wind up. It's more an exploration of the territory than a trip to a specific destination; more a process of discovering what we don't know than a process of applying what we do know. This is an important issue for business leaders who seek a more sustainable world, because the very nature of leadership can restrict our freedom of exploration and discovery.

In most businesses, leaders are people who are expected to get results. That's why they're out in front. People want to be organized and led by someone with demonstrated capability. Michael Dell started selling computers through mail order while he was still in college, and by the time he was in his early 20s, there were not many companies selling more personal computers than he was. Dell knew more about it, had more perspectives on it, and could lead others in his business model very effectively. Bill Gates never finished college, but his ability to tackle a complex software problem set him apart from other programmers and inspired those who followed him. In these two cases, it wasn't the level of education or erudition that made these men leaders. Michael Dell and Bill Gates got results, and still do. That's the essence of their success.

Because getting good results tends to overshadow everything else in business, leaders who have been successful over time are likely to rely on whatever actions got those results in the past. They may learn new management theories, or gain new communication skills. But their internal logic remains unchanged because it's so clear to them and so rewarding. As long as leaders who take this approach stay in businesses they understand, and there are no radical changes in technology or consumer behavior, they can continue getting results.

It's when things shift dramatically that this dependence on past actions becomes a liability. At a time when the world is crying out for a new approach, we need to remember the power of exploration and discovery. Technology changes faster than ever. Global market dynamics tend to amplify small movements in one place into tidal waves in another. Politics and human rights issues become harder to separate from economic and commercial considerations. Managers are constantly facing new challenges, new situations, and new pressures, and their successful actions of the past may not always prevail.

A business may already have world-beating expertise for researching new materials, developing innovative products, and finding new markets. To become a sustainable business, however, now it will be necessary to explore the larger system those activities take place in, and discover the interconnections. You may realize that for all the current success your business has, it's not sustainable for the long term. You may also realize that you just don't know, sitting here at this moment, how to change it.

THE STRENGTH IN "I DON'T KNOW"

BUSINESS LEADERS NEED TO SEE this uncertain state—not knowing—as the start of exploration and discovery, not as the end of our right to lead. That idea was sometimes hard when I first took over as president of Fetzer. Often a discussion would come around to something I believed we needed to do, and someone would ask, in either confusion or anticipation, "Well, how do we do that?" I would have to tell them I didn't know. This didn't always feel very good, for them or for me. The way to make it feel better was for me to make it clear that we were going to find out together. As a team, we were going to discover new ways of operating, even if we didn't know right now what they would turn out to be. Everyone on my Leadership Team had to go through a similar process, because their own people were looking at them and asking, "How?"

Today, it's different. Everyone at Fetzer knows to answer the question with "Let's go find out!" More important, I now believe that in our organization, people grant us more rights to leadership when we admit we don't know, and then everyone shifts right into the exploration and discovery mode. It's genuine. It's inclusive. It energizes people to do their own discovery and exploration rather than wait for answers. I believe this is absolutely essential to building a sustainable business, because at times you will need all the creativity you can muster.

Closely related to this aspect of sustainable leadership is creating space for your people to conduct their own exploration and discovery, without judgment and without limiting the answers they might come upon. In my wallet I carry a quote about leadership. I've never been able to find out who the author is, but whoever it is speaks clearly to me: "There are only two demands of leadership. One is to accept that rank does not confer privileges; it entails responsibility. The other is to acknowledge that leaders in an organization need to impose on themselves that congruence between deeds and words, between behavior and professed beliefs and values that we call personal integrity. In other words—walk their talk."

I may have gotten my rank and position from the board of directors of Brown-Forman, but I get the right to lead from the people of Fetzer Vineyards. This in turn means I have to practice what I preach and lead by example. I have to let them go on their own process of exploration and discovery. If I think I know where they should go, I can't just push them in that direction or limit what paths they take. If I tell them that "I don't know" is a strong position for me, I have to let it be a strong position for them, too.

I am still refining my ability to do this, and my six-year-old daughter Sassicaia helps with my education. When she was two years old, I taught her how to keep her balance on a pony. She was holding onto the reins, and I told her first to let go with one hand, then to let go with the other. That worked okay, so I told her to hold one arm straight out to the side. That worked too, and I told her to try it on the other side. Finally I said, "Okay, now hold both arms straight out at the same time." She gave me this look that said "No way!" I had an urge to convince her to do it anyway, but I let it pass and just waited. A moment later, she put both her arms out to the sides. I realized she had to explore her own balance in this strange new situation of sitting on a horse with her arms flung out to her sides. If I created the space for that exploration, she discovered what she needed and real progress followed.

It was the same in the swimming pool. If I didn't push her, she let her own interest and curiosity draw her on. She was just four when I noticed she was watching older kids jump off a ten-meter board. I asked her if she wanted to try it, and she gave me the "No way!" look. So I shrugged and we kept splashing around. A little while later she said, "I want to try it now." I told her I would be waiting in the water for her when she landed. So up she went, high over my head. When she got to the top, she walked out on the board, didn't hesitate at all, and dove!

When she came up, we swam over to the side and I could tell right away that she was not very happy. We climbed out, I dried her off and held her for a while. Finally she said, in a small voice, "That didn't feel very good." I gently asked her why. She said it hurt her eyes. This puzzled me for a moment. Then I asked, "Did you keep your eyes open when you dove in?" She nodded.

This, I submit, is a good lesson for leaders of sustainable businesses. The process of exploration and discovery works best when we keep our eyes wide open. Every now and then, it might not feel very good, but that temporary discomfort is far outweighed by new knowledge and greater courage. We come to understand that we can push back old boundaries, move into new territory, and create new possibilities. There is a growing sense that we can, indeed, work together across cultures and companies, across countries and communities, to preserve this precious Earth for ourselves and all future generations.

This book is Fetzer's contribution to that conversation.

FIRST PRINCIPLE

YOUR BUSINESS IS PART OF A MUCH LARGER SYSTEM

On November 19, 2002, I stood at the podium in a large meeting room at the Fairmont Hotel in San Francisco. Looking out at an unprecedented gathering of the leaders of the California wine community, I felt as if everything in my life was coming together in that moment. In a few minutes, a press conference would begin, announcing the creation of a Code of Sustainable Winegrowing Practices for California. I was there to speak as a member of the board of directors of the Wine Institute, which had partnered with the California Association of Winegrape Growers to create the code. We were going public with our commitment to make the wine industry an example for everyone in agriculture. Fetzer had played an influential role in bringing about this momentous occasion, and a powerful flood of emotion came over me.

I personally feel that wine is different from other products that people buy and consume. There is a romance to wine, and a mystery in the art that creates it. These qualities enable wine to engender lively discussions that make people want to learn more about it. This is one of the reasons why going public as an industry with a commitment to sustainability was an important moment. To a greater degree than other industries, we have a chance to change hearts and minds with our actions. I felt I was not only representing my fellow vintners and growers at this conference, I was speaking to consumers and to the wider world of all business. In my speech I said:

> *"If we can transform California viticulture, we can transform the world of viticulture. And if we can transform the world of viticulture, we can transform the world of agriculture. If our wine community can demonstrate the wisdom and viability of sustainable business practices, then the world business community itself will be able to see a new opportunity and responsibility that has the power to lead us to a thriving and sustainable world for all."*

My words capped a long journey of discovery, one that began in certainty, passed through a personal crisis full of doubt and pain, and finally arrived at this moment of new hope and possibility.

FINDING ROOTS AT FETZER

SOON AFTER I RECEIVED my graduate degree in winemaking, I interviewed with Fetzer Vineyards. Right off, I bonded with Barney Fetzer, the patriarch and founder of the family winery. He had purchased a run-down ranch in 1958 and turned it into a winery with the help of his wife and eleven children, so he had already set some deep roots in the land around his home. He had a passion for exploration and was eager to see what he could do with an ambitious, well-trained winemaker. I'm not sure he realized when he hired me how ambitious I was. In those days, I believed I could do anything.

That first harvest I made Gewürztraminer, Riesling, Chenin Blanc, and Sauvignon Blanc, all white wines that were new for Fetzer. I knew about them from my tastings at California State University at Fresno and I had wanted to try my hand at them. Barney was always willing to try something different. He would come in and say, "I've heard about some grapes down in Monterey, want to go get them?" My response was always, "Let's go!" It would be late in the season, we'd be in the middle of crush, there would be absolutely no room left in the winery, but I'd say yes anyway. In fact, if someone suggested, even remotely, that I couldn't or wouldn't be able to do something, my immediate internal response was, *I'll show you.* I was a very bull-headed young man.

My attitude was not a problem then, because the winery was still fairly small and family-run. Fetzer Vineyards needed someone willing to go all out. The market was surging in the 1980s. We caught the crest of the wine wave and began to grow like crazy. In 1982, we released our first Sundial Chardonnay, which today sells nearly a million cases a year. Sales were going through the roof. Everyone was working hard and being regularly rewarded for their efforts. Being somewhat stubborn and demanding seemed appropriate if we were going to rise to the opportunity in front of us. I expected more of myself than anyone. If I had to work another ten hours a week on top of everything else, I would do it, just to prove I was right. Just to prove I could.

There were signs early on that this management style was going to have consequences for Fetzer Vineyards and for my personal life. My second year at the winery, 1978, Barney made a special deal with American Airlines to provide it with Gamay Beaujolais for its in-flight passengers, which meant we would need to make more Gamay than the previous year. Of course I agreed. After all, this was one of Barney's favorite wines. I got to work and purchased Gamay Beaujolais from growers throughout Mendocino, crushed the grapes, and put them through their primary fermentation. This is the stage of winemaking in which the sugars in the grape juice are consumed by yeasts to produce alcohol. (For a more detailed description of winemaking, see pages 173–181.) Then comes a second fermentation, in which harsh malic acids in the grapes are converted by tiny bacteria into softer lactic acids. Malic acids are sharp, like the acids in apples, while lactic acids are soft, like the acids in milk. Malolactic fermentation, as it's known, both softens and stabilizes red wine, as long as the process is fully complete before you bottle. Otherwise, the wine keeps fermenting in the bottle, and when you open it you have an unpleasant surprise. It's often not even drinkable.

For this American Airlines Gamay, I was ready to bottle. The lab results suggested the wine might need a bit more time to go completely through malolactic fermentation. To my winemaker's sure palate, the wine seemed soft and stable enough to me when I tasted it, so I self-assuredly ordered it to be bottled. I knew that I could filter out any remaining lactic bacteria with a fine enough filter. But the winery didn't have such a filter, and I didn't go out and find one. I didn't think I needed it. I trusted my own judgment, despite the data.

You can guess what's coming. The wine started to ferment again in the bottle, after we had shipped it out. Obviously, American Airlines didn't want Gamay Beaujolais that was bubbling away in the bottle for its passengers. We had to pull all the wine from the airline, resulting in a serious financial loss to the family. We had a big opportunity with our 1978 Gamay Beaujolais to get the wine before an important audience and build a long and mutually rewarding relationship, and I failed. There is no way to measure the loss in terms of pride and Fetzer Vineyards' reputation. But at the time, I didn't apologize to Barney or anyone in the Fetzer family. I wouldn't even acknowledge my mistake. *Any* mistake.

Every serious winemaker has had a wine go bad for one reason or another. Wine is one of the most complex biological liquids on Earth, and although we are its makers, we are never quite its masters. So my experience with the Gamay Beaujolais was not unique. Yet I deflected responsibility for it with every excuse I could. We were growing, making lots of wine, and I was under a lot of pressure. I was making the Fetzer family a lot of money and bringing them all kinds of acclaim. How could they expect me to be perfect?

Fetzer's business was booming, sometimes doubling in size year over year. In some ways, the acknowledgment and the praise I was getting from Barney, from other winemakers, and from the marketplace made me think it was all I really needed. I can remember even saying at times that what I loved about crush was that I had absolutely no responsibility and no obligations to anyone but the wine. I was in my own world, and everyone else had to adjust to me.

When I joined Fetzer, I was married to a woman named Lynne. She was incredibly supportive of my dream of becoming a winemaker and a pioneer in what was then considered a remote winegrowing area. She also shared my passion for wine and made life easy wherever we lived. Her love was family, and she made the move to Redwood Valley a fun adventure for our two boys. But most of the time, I was having my own private adventure at the winery. That's where I was in my element, and that's where I spent the majority of my time.

Over the years, things became difficult at home and tense at the winery. People told me later that I walked around the winery with a scowl on my face all the time. I was probably the same with my family, but my wife and kids were afraid to tell me. Perhaps they did try to tell me, but I couldn't hear it. The formula of command and control that I had learned during three years in the military before I went to study winemaking, of setting and achieving goals by and for my own authority, no longer succeeded with the people I loved most in the world. Still, I could not abandon it. It had worked far too well, for far too long, for me to see what lay ahead. Finally, I shipwrecked my marriage and devastated my own family, and then it was too late. Lynne and I divorced in 1983. I was furious at others, furious at myself, and unable to express it. I still could not acknowledge my own role in the failure, which made it worse. I went through a dark period where it was hard to stay focused even on winemaking.

Fortunately, it didn't kill me or hurt the winery. I still had my work ethic, and I had managed to hire a few people whom I did finally trust and rely on. But I had to find some new bedrock to stand on. What I thought was a firm foundation had gone to quicksand. I started, perhaps for the first time, questioning myself and my motives. Wanting something firmer for my life took me into a new phase of questioning what was important to me, and why. Why was I was doing what I was doing? What did I really need to fulfill me? I sought counseling. I read books. I took courses. Slowly I got back to some semblance of normality. In 1986, I married for the second time to Diana Fetzer, a very special lady with whom I share many interests. We both love food and wine, and we love being outdoors in the garden (her) or the vineyard (me). She is the eighth of the eleven Fetzer children, and we had a picture-book wedding at the winery.

Around this time, Fetzer Vineyards had a string of incredible vintages, including the memorable, even historic ones of 1985, 1986, and 1987. I believe those wines, particularly the Cabernet Sauvignons, would still stand up to the best wines of the world. By 1988, however, I had to face the fact that no matter how good the wine was, I was still struggling with what was really important to me. As you can imagine, with this continuing confusion, my new marriage was rocky at times, which alternately scared me and angered me.

OPENING UP

IT WAS MY BROTHER PETER who finally helped me see that my personal drive for success at work was an empty substitute for discovering what really made me happy. My own judgments were more real to me than the behavior of the people around me, and justifying my own world was more important than joining the world everyone else was living in. I saw that I had not fulfilled my role as husband and father for my family. Rather than discovering who they were and what we needed to flourish together, I had simply taken what I needed from them and let them deal with the consequences, like a business that doesn't care about the consequences of polluting rivers or mistreating its workers.

It was the same with my winemaking team. I realized that I controlled and dominated them, using them to advance my own ambition, never allowing for their own personal growth or success.

I certainly rarely shared any recognition. I thought I was serving Fetzer, but I was, in reality, pursuing my own personal agenda. That gave me justification for getting angry at people rather than stopping to question my own part in the system, my own role in our success and occasional failure. This may be typical "leadership" behavior in many corporations, but that did not excuse it. The environment I created was one of uncertainty, hesitation, caution. I personally felt free to do whatever I wanted, but the people who reported to me obviously felt differently.

With this new awareness, I started to slowly change my behavior and create a more positive environment. Instead of expecting my winemaking team to fail or let me down, I opened up to them. Instead of enforcing my world on them, I found the world we inhabited together, where our communication could be a two-way street that offered more freedom of expression to everyone. After some initial doubt, they responded. The results were unbelievable.

The extent of the changes I'd made were brought home to me by the holiday season of 1991. December is also review time for winemakers. I'd met with and reviewed my team that particular morning. I was scheduled for my own review with John Fetzer (Barney's son, who was CEO at this time) late that same morning. The winemakers, somewhat inconveniently, wanted to take me to what they had hinted was a special lunch. I agreed, though it meant I would have to hope that my own review would be completed on time so I could rush from my meeting with John to head downtown to one of our favorite restaurants. I wondered, if only for a moment, if this might be a goodbye lunch for one of my team.

As I walked into the restaurant, the winemakers were hard to miss. There they sat, all five of them, grinning like Cheshire cats. They asked how the review had gone, and I said, "Well, I've got the fax machines sending out my résumé as we speak." This joke fell flat even as I heard the words come out of my mouth. I began to feel uneasy.

Just then, Dennis Martin, whom I consider one of my best friends, began speaking. "We just want to give you something special because you've been really great to us." He slid a handmade wooden box across the table. The gift was a winemaker's dream: a bottle of 1985 Château Mouton Rothschild. The box carried a small brass plaque: "Thanks For Your Guidance, Your Support, And Your Friendship." Receiving it is one of my favorite moments as a winemaker, a cherished memory that marks a great step forward in my life. I realized at that moment that I had truly changed. I was making a positive difference in the lives of my coworkers, and I also felt the wonderful impact they had made on my life. This was the payoff for the hard work of transformation I had begun some two years before.

As I came out of my own world and joined the rest of the world around me, I saw that there were many needs going unfulfilled and I began to wonder how I could make a larger difference than by simply making wines. I even played with the idea of going back to school and becoming a doctor. That way I could directly touch the lives of others and know at the end of each day what contribution I had made in the world.

But in 1992, the Fetzer family sold the winery to Brown-Forman and recommended that the new owners appoint me president. They agreed and suddenly, unexpectedly, the opportunity to make a bigger contribution to the world was opening up right in front of me. Around that same time, I read an eye-opening book called *The Ecology of Commerce* by Paul Hawken. His analogy—that the world of business could work with the same harmony and balance as the natural world—deeply appealed to me. Already, with the help of my brother, I was making a personal transition from living in my own world to living fully in the larger world around me, and that had enabled me to make a difference in my relationships with others. Now, through Hawken's book, I began to imagine that I could do the same thing with Fetzer. Our whole company could operate with a far richer awareness of its place in the world, and from that perspective it could make a much bigger difference than I could make alone.

Ten years later, I now see this as the first principle for sustainable business: *Your business is part of a much larger system.*

REDEFINING PROGRESS

THE VIEW OF OUR FOREFATHERS in business was that continuous economic growth is the natural path for human progress. Ongoing technological advancement increases productivity, and the development of new products improves the quality of life. Economic globalization spurs competition, creates jobs, improves the conditions of developing countries, and is, in general, a benefit to all.

This is a great story, and it's a complete story if you accept the original premise, that human progress comes from continuous economic growth. We now know, as Hawken was already arguing a decade ago, that left to its own unconscious devices, continuous economic growth produces the reverse of progress. It is actually endangering the earth we all share.

Humanity now consumes resources and produces waste faster than the earth can replenish and absorb them. One of the indicators that the United Nations monitors is known as the "ecological footprint" of human activity. This metric was created by an organization called Redefining Progress. It involves a tremendous amount of research and analysis, all to give us a simple, powerful way to understand our impact on the earth. The latest "ecological footprint" update, in November 2002, calculates that our biosphere currently needs about a year and three months to renew the resources and absorb the waste that humanity consumes and throws away in a year.

In other words, we're using up fifteen months of the earth for every twelve months of real time. We're behaving as if we had more than one Earth to live on. We're living beyond our means. We're borrowing from the future, accelerating toward the day when Earth simply won't be able to sustain humanity any longer. This is particularly sobering when you learn that a third of the 6.2 billion people on Earth live on the equivalent of less than one dollar a day. So even as we're drawing down the planet's reserves, we're leaving billions of people far from the wealth we've created. Is it any wonder their anger and resentment are rising?

I still believe in economic growth, but I no longer see it as separate from everything else going on in the world. I now believe that business can change its premise and view economic growth from a larger perspective. If we start from the position that our businesses are part of a much larger system, we see success and failure differently. If my business helps keep the system healthy and vibrant, my business benefits. If the system fails, then my business fails too.

At Fetzer, we now recognize certain realities shape everything we go. Here are some:

- **We are not alone**: Everyone, and every business, inhabits the same larger system. None of us is outside it or exempt from its realities.

- **We are not separate**: All our actions as a company and as individuals affect the larger system, just as its health and well-being affect us. Everything within the larger system is interconnected and interdependent.
- **We can make a difference**: The choices we make can turn interconnectedness into a lever long enough to move the world. We can create change in the larger system by how we operate in our own spheres of influence—whether it's inside our companies, inside our communities, or inside our industries.

This thought—that your business is part of a much larger system—does not in any way diminish the power, resources, and potential of business to create wealth and progress. The new possibility is to harness business's efficiency and innovation, its sheer ability to focus people's attention, to leverage our interconnectedness rather than ignore it. Business should do more than just maximize profits.

PUTTING THE PRINCIPLE OF INTERCONNECTEDNESS INTO PRACTICE

ONCE WE ACCEPT that we're sharing the limited resources of this planet together, the next step is to see that what affects one affects us all. We expect the managers of multinational corporations to think globally, but now everyone feels the interconnections that ripple around the globe. Even the owner of a mom-and-pop grocery store knows that the prices and demand for certain products are caused by what happens halfway around the world. A government decision to plant coffee beans in Vietnam brings down a decades-old system of coffee pricing between North and South America, driving thousands of coffee workers to the brink of poverty. Deregulation of energy delivery in California throws the energy industry out of whack in the entire American West. Regional economies are more affected than ever by the global macroeconomy, and policy makers are increasingly losing their ability to manage separate national destinies.

Beyond the large, visible consequences of interconnectedness are the invisible consequences. There is not a single person on Earth, I believe, who ever wanted to create a hole in the ozone layer. Yet all of us together have created such a hole. A layer of molecules made from oxygen atoms, floating thousands of miles up in the atmosphere, seems about as remote from our life as anything could be, even less a part of our daily experience than the moon. Yet the ozone layer is a vital filter that moderates the sun's energy. It's one of the reasons life evolved on this beautiful, temperate planet. Through a large number of unaware but interconnected actions, we have created an unintended and undesired result.

Once we see that we are part of a much larger system, and that we are interconnected with everything within it, we can start to have a more positive influence. When scientists discovered the role of chlorofluorocarbons (CFCs) in stripping oxygen molecules out of the atmosphere, it enabled us to change our behavior and ban or limit the release of CFCs into the atmosphere.

This same process applies to business. First, we must be aware that our businesses are part of a much larger system. This awareness needs to start at the top, so people take it seriously. Out of that awareness we naturally can see the interconnections, and the opportunities where a change in our business practices will lead to new and better consequences for the system. Finally, we can respond to those opportunities by acting, and through those actions create sustainable businesses for a sustainable world.

GAINING AWARENESS

FOR THE PAST TEN YEARS, we've been learning how this process works at Fetzer Vineyards. Many of our vineyards lie alongside the Russian River, and we noticed the potential for erosion of topsoil and road cuts to silt up streams that fish rely on for reproduction. We realized that what we called "the creek" flowing through our winery was not just a drainage ditch but a critical part of the ecosystem, a large, complex watershed inhabited by many living things. Because of development, our new vineyards were closer to housing and industrial areas, not located well out into the country as the original ones had been. We now have more neighbors and more animals competing for the same space. After a while, it was impossible to see anything related to our work with the land that was not part of a much larger system.

We also became more aware that Fetzer is one of the largest employers in our economically depressed county. We had seen other local businesses failing, most notably timber and fishing. We had seen the devastating impact these business failures had on our area. It was crystal clear that Fetzer Vineyards' economic success was critical to the quality of life in the community and that the people who worked for our company were the same people who lived in the surrounding towns. We saw that we had influence. We had a responsibility. We took a look at how we compensated our employees relative to other companies, how we housed vineyard workers relative to other wineries, and how we interacted with our community compared to other businesses.

Our place in the economic system was something we talked about all the time, but thinking about the larger system gave us fresh perspectives. If we were going to keep growing at the rate we intended, we needed a lot more grapes, from a lot farther away, and we needed to get much better at the logistics of finding them and bringing them to our winery. We had to be sure that we found suppliers and vendors that supported our business practices. We were going to have to be able to keep hiring top-quality people in a thinly populated rural area. So, we would either have to recruit them from other communities or develop a training program strong enough to build talent from within. We were going to have to expand our distribution channels and reach more consumers, convincing them to drink Fetzer wine because of its quality and inherent value. We wanted consumers to know about our sustainable practices, so those who shared our views would have yet another reason to buy our wine.

In short, all our plans involved the outside world. If we didn't manage our interconnection to it, we were not going to be successful financially.

RESPONDING TO OPPORTUNITIES TO OPERATE MORE SUSTAINABLY

AS WE HAVE OPENED UP our awareness of our larger system, the opportunities to operate Fetzer more sustainably seem to arise nonstop. One that we have embraced most fully is stewardship of the earth. This stewardship includes all our own vineyards, old and new. It involves proactive restoration and conservation: eliminating chemicals; planning how and where we lay out new vineyards; changing how we irrigate our fields; determining where we site roads and allow vehicles; committing to conserve and restore riparian habitat. We also have influence and impact on thousands of additional acres due to our grape purchasing contracts with other growers, and we are working with them so they will farm their fields sustainably, as well.

Beyond that, our commitment to the land is helping shape an industry-wide conversation about sustainable agricultural practices. We also see an opportunity to help conserve resources, so we are constantly reducing our energy use per unit of output, reducing solid and liquid waste, and increasing the percentage of energy we generate or purchase from renewable sources.

Seeing our people as the living link between Fetzer and the community has led to an equally strong commitment to change how the winery relates to both. We have transformed our worker housing program, sponsored ESL programs for our Spanish-speaking workers, and helped employees find full expression for their leadership skills, not just at work but in the community, as well. We have opened up our organic garden and culinary programs for local educators, created scholarship programs, and donated money and employee time to numerous local community causes.

We are also actively sharing everything we have learned and done to make Fetzer more sustainable. We're connecting with the wine industry and the broader business community. This is now making a difference in the way our industry works—a difference that can be a model for all agriculture, everywhere. That model includes equitable treatment for people, preservation of the earth's natural vitality, and a solid economic return for business owners.

TAKING UP THE MANTLE FOR SUSTAINABLE VITICULTURE

ONE OF THE WAYS we became a leader was by committing Fetzer to grow only organic grapes. Our own vineyards include about 2,000 acres, which is a drop in the bucket in a state with half a million acres under vines. But our stand for organic viticulture captured the attention of many growers and vintners, who see a major opportunity to reposition the wine industry as a caretaker of the earth rather than another example of so-called "industrial farming."

California's Wine Institute, which represents hundreds of wineries producing the vast majority of the state's wine, and the California Association of Winegrape Growers, which represents the state's large community of independent grape growers, have now taken up the mantle for sustainable viticulture, educating their members and informing the public. That's what led to the creation of the Code of Sustainable Winegrowing Practices. This in turn is sending ripples beyond the wine industry, because as the wine industry shifts toward sustainable farming, it's going to become an example to the rest of the state's huge agricultural sector—and to millions of consumers throughout the country.

THE WINE INDUSTRY STEPS UP

IN 1999, BILL TURRENTINE, a well-regarded California grape and wine broker, posed a provocative question: Should the American wine community have a vision for the future? The timing of his question was good, because the industry was healthy and in a good position to consider its future. Furthermore, Bill saw that other large wine-producing nations—particularly Australia—were aiming directly at the U.S. market. The corporate-led Aussie wine business had already proven that it could produce a quality product in high volumes at a very competitive price, due to lower costs for land and production and favorable exchange rates.

Now the Australians were planting vineyards at an escalating pace, as part of a strategic plan to become a major player in the worldwide wine market. Chile, Argentina, and New Zealand were also planting at levels nobody had ever seen before. France, Italy, and other "Old World" wine countries were continuing to expand their vineyard and winemaking research efforts with the support of government subsidies. California had doubled its planted acres in the 1990s, so we also were going to have a lot more wine to sell. Where would it all go?

So I helped to put together a meeting of 60 wine industry leaders from around America, representing over 95 percent of the wine produced in the United States. Called the Wine Vision meeting, it was an incredible event in many ways. The wine industry in this country has historically been made up of independent producers who don't normally work together on projects. In fact, most of the people at this meeting were known for being fiercely independent. (I suppose you could count me in that bunch.) Everyone was learning what other people thought about things, often for the first time.

DEVELOPING A VISION

YOU MIGHT EXPECT that 60 fiercely independent people would come up with 60 fiercely opposed opinions. It turned out that there was an amazing amount of alignment. And by the end of the second day, we developed a vision for America's wine industry. Our strategic intent was that America would be the preeminent supplier in the global marketplace, in which there are established giants, such as France and Italy, and emerging powerhouses, such as Australia and South America. Gaining market leadership in such a setting would be challenging, but we felt it was achievable. Three strategic platforms would get us there.

First, we would participate in the markets that demonstrated the greatest potential for growth and prosperity. That's just good business, but we needed to articulate it and develop a plan that would focus our resources. Most of us had less than ten years' experience in the global market, so we were just beginning to understand the dynamics of international trade, regional cultures, and global marketing techniques and consumer interest. Second, we would make wine a part of American culture. This was more intriguing. It would require us to shift the cultural perspective that the American public had about wine. We want them to know what we know—that wine can be a part of a healthy, responsible lifestyle. Consider the differences in wine attitudes and consumption levels between the United States and Europe: Europeans treat wine as food and drink it in moderation with meals, while most Americans consider wine an alcoholic beverage. This is a big reason that healthy per capita consumption of wine is much higher in Europe than it is in the United States.

It was the third platform everyone agreed on that floored me:

The American wine industry would become a leader in sustainable business.

Looking back, I'm still surprised. I did not go into the meeting determined to put sustainability on the agenda. Yet when the topic came up, people looked at me and expected me to speak. Apparently they had been reading and hearing about how Fetzer was doggedly determined to run its business on a sustainable basis. They considered us leaders. We were not aware of the influence we were having on the whole conversation about where the wine business should go, but in the real, literal discussion over those two days, sustainability took center stage. Other people with interest in and experience on the subject then spoke up, and it became part of the whole wine community's goal-setting.

Soon after that Wine Vision meeting, the Wine Institute and the California Association of Winegrape Growers formed a partnership and began writing a Code of Sustainable Winegrowing Practices. Fetzer, along with other industry leaders and professionals, contributed information and advice on all aspects of viticulture and wine production, human resources, community relations, and corporate citizenship. The code is now being introduced to vintners and growers throughout California, and it will have a meaningful impact in the years to come.

All of this activity culminated for me at that point on the podium in 2002. I felt that my whole career had led me to that special moment. It's amazing to look back now at my original, very singular and personal desire to make a bigger contribution to the world and see how it has expressed itself, through my job and my company. I didn't know, when I was named president of Fetzer, that it could become a model for a whole industry, spanning many nations. I didn't know that one person's desire to contribute more could help create an environment for countless other people to express their own desire to make a contribution. Now I see that we're interconnected, part of a much larger, ever-changing system. And we can make a difference.

SECOND PRINCIPLE

YOUR COMPANY'S CULTURE IS DETERMINED BY THE CONTEXT YOU CREATE FOR IT

A good friend of mine, a management consultant, once told me the following story.

I was consulting for the management team of a hospital. They were looking for ways to improve customer service. I was on the project for more than a week and had interviewed over 50 people, becoming familiar with their duties and responsibilities. I was looking for that certain something that would inspire everyone at the hospital to have the spirit that management wanted them to have. Just learning everyone's jobs and understanding what role each person played was a big task.

After working late one night at the hospital, I was tired and eager to get home to relax. As I was heading for the door I saw an older gentleman in overalls very carefully mopping the floors. I really didn't want to stop, but he was an employee of the hospital after all, and I had not talked to any janitors yet. I decided to ask him a couple of quick questions.

> *It wouldn't take long, because in my own mind I knew what his job was and what he did: he mopped floors after everyone else was gone. He was the janitor.*
>
> *Nonetheless, as I approached him, he stopped and looked up and gave me a welcoming smile. I introduced myself and asked if I could speak with him, and he graciously obliged. My first question was the standard opening: Can you tell me what your job is?*
>
> *He paused for a moment, and then proudly said, "I help Dr. Johnson save lives."*

I can remember my friend telling this story like it was yesterday. It had an impact that I hope never leaves me. All I could imagine was our people at Fetzer. If a janitor mopping floors could see himself as part of a team that saved lives, I wanted Fetzer's vineyard workers, production people, sales people, and everyone else in the company, including me, to see themselves as part of a team that had a higher purpose, too.

This story also helped me understand the extent to which people want their work to stand for more than just a paycheck. They want the hours and days and years they put into working to amount to something more personal than a corporate bottom line. It doesn't have to be idealistic—it just has to have value to them personally. Consider this passage that appeared in a *Harvard Business Review* article from 1996:

> *I want to discuss why a company exists in the first place, in other words, why are we here? I think many people assume, wrongly, that a company exists simply to make money. While this is an important result of a company's existence, we have to go deeper and find the real reasons for our being... You can look around and see people who are interested in money and nothing else, but the underlying drives come largely from a*

> *desire to do something else: to make a product, to give a service—generally to do something which is of value.*

This was part of a speech given in 1960 by David Packard, one of the founders of Hewlett-Packard. For Packard and cofounder Bill Hewlett, a business had to stand for something more than just making money. The purpose they created was so strong at their company it engendered an enduring culture known in the business world as "the HP Way." One of the main reasons Hewlett's son Walter opposed HP's merger with Compaq in 2001 was that he believed the consequences of the merger, including large-scale layoffs to fit a certain cost structure, would not be part of the HP Way. His opposition to the merger was not based on the financials, it was based on remaining true to the company's roots.

We accept without question that philanthropic or service organizations can organize entirely to fulfill a purpose that inspires people. The Peace Corps is a great example. People will go to third world countries and work around the clock at things they would never do at home, because it serves a higher purpose. They're not doing it for the money. They're traveling thousands of miles from home to teach agricultural self-sufficiency to villagers in Africa to experience what it means to make a contribution to the world.

I see no reason why people should not find that same experience when they show up for work every day, no matter where they work. There should be no reason any group of people cannot organize themselves around the twin goals of making money and making a difference.

During the dot-com explosion, we read and heard endlessly that people flocked to all the new Internet-based companies because they wanted to become millionaires. It now appears that many people made the choice as much for personal meaning as for money. At a company level, they saw a chance to create a new industry, revolutionize old industries, and eliminate unnecessary layers between people and the fulfillment of their desires. Those are big missions. At a personal level, they saw a chance to fully express their creativity and imagination in a much more individual, entrepreneurial way.

It's not hard to understand why people who came through that brief, electrifying era find it hard to go back to jobs without any apparent larger value attached. Many are moving into service work. Brilliant code writers are becoming teachers. People who used to create strategic partnerships are applying what they learned about the Internet to advance human rights or health care for the elderly or resource conservation. What gives their new jobs meaning is not just the money they earn from the work, but also the purpose of the work itself.

That's what I wanted for Fetzer: a higher purpose that would enable us to make a difference beyond crafting high quality wines at a great price. To get there, I knew I needed to have everyone aligned with this purpose, just like the janitor was aligned with the hospital's higher purpose. I had to find that guiding light that would engage everyone in the organization in a compelling way. I knew we had to come at it from the perspective of being part of a larger system, and I knew it would take exploration and discovery. And as soon as I could, I launched that process.

DISCOVERING OUR PURPOSE AT FETZER

WHEN THE FETZER FAMILY sold the winery to Brown-Forman Corporation, the Fetzer siblings chose to leave the management positions they had held for many of the winery's 24 years to seek new challenges and adventures. I went from head of winemaking to president of the company. The other people at Fetzer who stepped into management with me are exceptional individuals, and that was a huge plus for Fetzer. It was also important for me personally. Among other things, it gave me confidence that I could realize my personal vision of finding a platform in business to help make the world a better place. At the same time, we were all facing significant challenges in our own departments and as a newly formed Leadership Team.

I had this incredible sense of urgency. I wanted to get started right away. One of the things that inspired this, frankly, was that Fetzer Vineyards was now owned by another company. Some on the new Leadership Team simply wanted to keep building the company we had been working on for years. I personally wanted our purpose to combine growth and profitability with making a difference in the world, and I knew I needed to get complete alignment on that purpose with Fetzer's new corporate parent.

Two months after the acquisition, I gathered the seven members of our Leadership Team and three leaders from Brown-Forman for a long weekend retreat. We hardly knew each other. I'm not at all sure what these corporate folks from Louisville, Kentucky, and the laid-back winemakers of Northern California expected from each other that first weekend. I sure didn't know exactly what to expect from the process we were about to undertake.

I found a remote homestead deep in the forests of northern Mendocino on the shores of Leonard Lake. There were two old Victorian homes, hidden some 20 miles off the main roads and sitting alongside this beautiful mountain lake ringed by towering old-growth redwoods. This setting was idyllic and inspiring, but also extremely rustic. There was no electricity. There would be no

PowerPoint presentations or laptop computers. It rained the entire time we were there, which meant our meetings were conducted by flashlight and kerosene lamp. I wondered, at times, if this was an omen for the future.

We spent the first part of the weekend getting to know each other, learning about our businesses and establishing our relationship. The time finally arrived to begin exploring a future direction for Fetzer Vineyards. We started by asking ourselves one seemingly simple question: "Why are we in business?"

The obvious answers came quickly, and were what you would expect. We were in business to produce quality wine. To make money. To grow the business. But I wanted to go deeper and kept asking, "Why?" People were tired of answering the question, or felt they had answered it already. Some tried to change the subject. We began arguing for the sake of arguing. Our discussions became more heated, and alliances formed and reformed around different concepts and ideas. The atmosphere was becoming uncomfortable. But we were stuck deep in the woods with nothing to do but define Fetzer's future. And I kept asking the question. Again and again: "Why are we in business?"

Eventually we discovered we actually had a lot of agreement about what we wanted for Fetzer. We were all passionately committed to being stewards of the brand. Growing volume and profitability was a given. Producing great quality wines at a good price was seen as a cornerstone of success, now and for the future. We all wanted to provide a great work environment for Fetzer people. We wanted to build relationships with our consumers and partner with our distributors. We wanted to market our wines in a socially responsible manner, and farm our land responsibly. There was a lot that was important, and all of it was critical to our success.

Our reason for being in business was ultimately summed up in one core purpose: *Fetzer people, enhancing the quality of life.*

In that phrase there was room for everything we did: farming, winemaking, finance and sales. We could enhance the quality of life for people who pop the cork on a bottle of Fetzer wine with dinner. We could enhance the quality of the life of the earth that gives us the grapes to make our wine. We could enhance the quality of life for everyone who gave their energy and passion in the creation and sale of the wines. Once we identified our purpose, there were opportunities everywhere we looked. We had just focused the lens through which we would view our company. Profit, growth, and quality goals all took on a different meaning.

As exhausted as we were after days of talking, we followed through by crafting a mission statement.

> *We are an environmentally and*
> *socially conscious grower, producer*
> *and marketer of wines of the*
> *highest quality and value.*
>
> *Working in harmony and with*
> *respect for the human spirit, we are*
> *committed to sharing information*
> *about the enjoyment of food*
> *and wine in a lifestyle of*
> *moderation and responsibility.*
>
> *We are dedicated to the*
> *continuous growth and development*
> *of our people and our business.*

One of the fascinating things about this mission statement to me now is how far we had journeyed in our process of discovery in just three days. "We are an environmentally and socially conscious grower, producer and marketer of wines of the highest quality and value" basically said in one sentence that we were going to place our environmental and social concerns on the same level with our business-oriented, economic goals of quality and value. Six years after this meeting, John Elkington published *Cannibals with Forks: the Triple Bottom Line of 21st Century Business.* This is the book that popularized the "triple bottom line" concept, which advocates that your financial results are not the only bottom-line impact you have on your stakeholders. Your other two bottom lines are the physical environment and social environment in which you operate. It's a powerful equation for sustainable businesses, and we committed to it implicitly in 1992.

A commitment to enhancing the quality of life just naturally gave rise to a context of making a contribution. We could add to the lives of our consumers by improving the quality and value of the wines we sell every year. We could become more fully engaged in our communities. Our organic farming was helping us manage Fetzer's environmental impact. We could contribute to the wine industry by openly sharing and advocating for our best practices. Probably the most important difference we could make was allowing our employees to fully express their own greatness and potential. Shoveling soggy, slippery grape skins out of a fermentation tank is hard, messy, even dangerous work, but if the context for it is to make the world a better place, then it's worthwhile, even important. If everyone in the winery sees his work in that light, then a culture of pride, quality, and hard work just naturally rises up from the workers themselves.

It was in noticing this intersection of purpose, context, and culture that the second principle of sustainable leadership began to show up for me: *The culture of your business is determined by the context you create for it.*

PURPOSE GIVES RISE TO CONTEXT

IN THE STORY my friend tells about the hospital, the janitor speaks with conviction about what happens at his hospital. Dr. Johnson is saving lives, and the janitor is helping him save lives. That's their shared purpose. This purpose creates a context for everything they do, from making appointments for patients to conducting open-heart surgery. Mopping floors may not be the most glamorous job, but if it is appreciated for providing sanitary conditions that help save lives, wouldn't anyone want to do the best job possible? That personal, value-based reaction—wanting to do the best job possible—arises directly from the hospital's context, and it becomes part of the culture.

Most businesses claim they have a clear purpose, but I would suggest that many business leaders are unaware that their purpose gives rise to context, and that the context is determining the culture of their company in a fundamental way. If the leader of an enterprise isn't intentionally creating the context, then the people in the enterprise are probably operating in some unintended context. The meaning and value of their work is being either supported by the context or dragged down by it, but the leaders don't know which.

When people really know what their context is, their work has meaning and the culture gets stronger. The culture becomes a living fulfillment of the purpose. If people don't have a clear context, because their leaders don't, it's hard to do more than show up, put in your time, punch the clock, and pick up a check. That seems to *be* the context: getting paid for time at work, regardless of how that time is spent. If that's the context, workers are unlikely to go all out. They just don't have a context that makes their work meaningful and fulfilling.

The purpose for most business today usually comes down to improving the financial bottom line and boosting the stock price or increasing shareholder value. It is generally expressed in ways you have heard before: Dominate the Category! Crush the Competition! Be Number 1! However it gets expressed, the context for people's activities inside the business tends to be the same: cutting costs, increasing sales, and improving profitability.

This has become the dominant context for business because delivering more profit quarter after quarter, year after year, truly does attract shareholders. Leaders who can say, "For the last x quarters, we've continually improved our profitability," have reason to be proud of that accomplishment. I certainly want to be able to say that about Fetzer. It's just that money alone is not enough of a context to motivate people on a sustained basis.

CONTEXT GIVES RISE TO CULTURE

I BELIEVE THAT THE RIGHT CULTURE can do anything, including building a sustainable business that's a powerful investor magnet. As leaders, our job is to cultivate our people, bringing out their best, and create a rich, human whole greater than the sum of the parts. That's culture: something bigger than the individuals within a group, which they nevertheless are an integral part of. Teamwork becomes more natural, because everyone knows why the work the next person is doing is valuable. If they're talking about that context all the time, if they are constantly looking at their workplace, their products, and their processes from the standpoint of fulfilling themselves and their purpose, you can hardly keep up with the ideas they bring forth.

I don't believe there is a generic context that is right for everyone. Every organization is unique, just as every person is unique. The context is going to be different for every single organization, and you have to discover it. That can take some work, as we found out at Leonard Lake. You have to plunge in and trust that the people with you will also plunge in, helping to identify your purpose for being in business. You have to articulate that purpose in a powerful, meaningful way so people get aligned with purpose. Then you know that the context that arises will be the right one for your organization, and it will take hold in many unforeseen ways.

STRAIGHT TALKS AND FUN TOURS

AFTER OUR RETREAT, the Leadership Team came back to the winery with a clear purpose and a mission statement that had the potential for everyone to participate. I see now how critical it was that we got going with implementation right away. Like many companies, we could have hung our mission statement on a wall, touted our purpose at company meetings, and then slowly allowed them to get elbowed aside by the more pressing task of hitting that quarterly profit number. Perhaps because we were so new to senior management that did not happen.

We soon realized that we would need to do three things right out of the box. First, we had to enroll our people in the new purpose, so they would begin to respond to the context it set for them. Second, we had to translate it into action so people could have tangible experiences based on making a contribution while fulfilling the purpose. Third, we had to start figuring out how to make those two processes, of buying into a purpose and expressing it through action, take on a life of their own.

Presenting Fetzer Vineyards' new purpose to the people in the company was not exactly a slam dunk. "Enhancing the quality of life" was actually a shock to some people. The sales team, especially, thought Fetzer Vineyards' purpose was making and selling great wine. Those activities were still important, but now they were just one part of the description of how we would fulfill our purpose. Other people loved the sound of our purpose but weren't exactly sure what it meant. Clearly, we were not going to enroll people in the purpose by telling them simply to get with it. Ultimately, we drew again on our process of exploration and discovery. Instead of management telling everyone what the purpose was, we made opportunities for them to tell us what *Fetzer people, enhancing the quality of life* meant to them.

This wasn't easy, for me anyway. I didn't become a leader by being bashful. I took control and made decisions. Wasn't that what I was being paid for? In the sustainable company I was advocating, I had to adjust my style of leadership. I had to be part of a shared process of discovery that didn't have a defined end point. I had to let the company lead me as much as I was leading the company. This was uncharted territory for all of us.

So I started spending time talking to people, in small groups. I wanted them to feel comfortable and confident enough to talk to me straight up. These conversations became known as "Straight Talks." I would gather a group of employees from one department, and just sit down for a few hours and talk. For employees, Straight Talks gave those who hadn't had much contact with me some time to get to know and trust me. Some took advantage of the opportunity to complain, which was fine. I'd rather have them complain to me, someone who could do something about it, than complain to their coworkers who could only internalize the negativity. In Straight Talks, people could ask me anything. Sometimes I didn't know the answer, and sometimes they didn't like the answer. The important thing was that we were talking honestly about the questions. I was able to share insights about the business and our future, and I was able to demonstrate how they fit into that future.

I also started leading what we called "Fun Tours" of Fetzer for small groups of workers. On Fun Tours, I got to show people the rest of the business they were part of, including our new winery, our vineyards, and the hospitality center and organic garden at Valley Oaks Ranch. This allowed people to see beyond their own department and start to see the value of their contribution inside a larger purpose. During the tour, I would talk to them about elements of the business, from sales reports to new products to new vineyard plantings and projected growth. Eventually, I would talk to them about our core purpose and desire as an organization to make contributions in many areas. Then we would have a great lunch, share some of our wine, and talk about what was most important to them in working for Fetzer Vineyards.

While this time with people was intended to help me enroll them in the purpose, Straight Talks and Fun Tours taught me as much as I taught anyone else. I learned that even though we had not done any grand communication of the purpose, or rolled out our plans or philosophies, most people knew what was important to us. This was very satisfying to me because it meant we were living it out, even if we had just figured it out. But I also learned that many people still didn't feel empowered and integrated. For every office worker who now saw his spreadsheet as integral to the purpose of the business, there was one who was just plugging in numbers. It was not that there was a lack of caring, it was because there was no context for the work being done. They didn't know they were helping Dr. Johnson save lives.

I was amazed what great ideas were rooted in the creative minds of our employees. I learned that a passion for the company, for what we did and how we did it, was not just in the management team or me—people felt it throughout the organization. Our workers had the same sense of pride and ownership in Fetzer as I did. I had to earn the leadership of this company, because it was just as much the workers' company as it was mine. In fact, we still have a large number of employees who believe that it is they who have entrusted Brown-Forman with the care of their company, not the other way around.

It took me a couple of years to share a Straight Talk with everyone in the company, but that time was well worth it. Straight Talks continue today, some led by me, some led by other managers or supervisors. They will always be a valuable part of our culture. But it was those first few years that put our mission in context for everyone. After that, it wasn't just the viticulturalists who were taking our vineyards organic, it was every one of us. It wasn't just the salespeople who were breaking records every year, it was everyone at Fetzer. It wasn't just our head winemaker who was winning medals and high ratings for our wines, it was everyone. Everything we did was a win for everyone.

SETTING THE CONTEXT THROUGH RESULTS

THE OTHER IMMEDIATE STEP we took to implement our purpose was to set up projects inside the business that would make a tangible difference, so that employees could see their results. These had to be projects that went to the heart of the business in some way, so people could begin to broaden their context from what they were doing already. And the projects had to be visible expressions of our purpose of enhancing the quality of life.

Fortunately, we had plenty of ideas to work with, starting with an expansion of our organic farming program. We were already proud of what we had accomplished in that area, with hundreds of acres of organic vineyards. We also felt strongly that the great fruit those vineyards produced gave us a competitive advantage in the marketplace. The grapes from these organic vineyards made great quality wines. So expanding that aspect of our business was immediately understandable to people on a business level, and they also knew that it was better for the earth.

Buying more organic grapes and producing more Bonterra wine (which we created in the 1980s and first distributed in 1991) was one project that jump-started a lot of people right away. A related project was to create packaging for the Bonterra wines that was environmentally friendly, using recycled paper and soy-based inks. A small number of people worked on this but the result was visible to thousands, both inside and outside Fetzer.

One of the other early projects didn't look to some people like it came out of our core business, but it really did. During our rapid growth period of the 1980s, we had, without thinking about it, also experienced geometric growth in waste that had to be hauled to landfills—in 1991 it was more than 1,700 cubic yards, and we paid for every single yard that left the winery. Cutting back waste meant money back in our pocket. It was also something that everyone in the company could relate to. Many of us already recycled at home, so it was not hard to get people thinking along the same lines at work. The man I picked for the challenge was Patrick Healy. He had been a recycling coordinator for a while, so I thought he'd be a good candidate. He certainly was on board with the environmental mission.

Little did I know just how far Patrick would run with his new assignment as the garbage guru. He examined our garbage analytically to see what we were throwing away. He instituted a broader company-wide recycling program. He found avenues for recycling things that were not easy to recycle. He met with department managers to go over what they were bringing in and why. He challenged them to send materials back to their vendors for reuse, or to do without it in the first place. If we needed big ideas, Patrick had them. If we needed small details run to ground, he nailed them. In the first year of Patrick's garbage guidance we reduced our landfill waste, and were presented with our first award from the California Waste Reduction Awards Program (WRAP). Since then we have received nine WRAP awards. In 2002, our production facilities sent less than 40 cubic yards to the landfill—less than 3 percent of the 1,700 cubic yards we started with.

There were a number of other projects, including wastewater reduction and reuse, and making the organic garden more of a community resource. In retrospect, it's interesting to me that all these early projects meant to help set a new context for Fetzer are still ongoing. We're still expanding our organic viticulture movement through our contract growers (all our estate vineyards are organically farmed today), and we're still looking for ways to cut the last few cubic yards of solid waste. All Fetzer wines and packaging are now benefiting from what Fetzer did with Bonterra.

LEADERSHIP'S ROLE

THE THIRD STEP in implementing our purpose and setting a context was figuring out how to make people's personal connection to the purpose, and their active expression of it, self-sustaining for the long term. Here we were on less solid ground. Talking to the employees was something we knew how to do. Assigning them projects was also something we knew how to do. Managing a brand new business with a brand new *approach* to business was a bit more of a challenge, and we had to develop our own style to find our way through it. Our entire Leadership Team was stepping into levels and areas of responsibility that were new for each person. Perhaps the lesson for sustainable businesses is, learn to forget the system and create your own.

We created ours by meeting regularly to have structured conversations about leadership. This was my "I don't know" period. Sometimes I did know what I wanted to do, or what I thought was right, but it was more important to get everyone involved than it was to tell them how it was going to be. So we talked, listened, expressed, debated, and argued. It was frustrating at times and discouraging when we failed. But we kept at it. I'm not sure if we clearly understood what we were doing, and what impact it would have. None of us had ever engaged in anything like this. Looking back, it's no wonder that we made mistakes, hit dead ends, and started over multiple times. But it was a conversation that we had to have. It was about our purpose, our whole context, and it was important to us. We were determined to live it out—whatever that meant.

Part of our discovery process was checking in with the wider world of management theories on a regular basis. I designated myself as the reader of management books and tester of management theories. I would bring in ideas from books from other companies or from *Harvard Business Review* and try them out on the team. I see now that this was an attempt to be the source of the answer, to know what we should do next. We would discuss these ideas, and sometimes we would try one or the other, but what ultimately became clear was that the team had a healthy skepticism about theories and formulas that were nicely packaged up. The way forward for us always seemed to be an internal process of discovery and trusting our people to respond to the purpose in their own way.

Back in the early 1990s, for example, it seemed every company was into values in a big way. At one point we thought we should do what we saw everyone else doing, which was write down some core values. We came up with things like respect, caring, and integrity. Nice words, very aspirational, but pretty generic. Then I discovered a great article by Jim Collins that advised companies not to make up or impose values that people were supposed to have. Instead, we should ask the culture to tell us what values it *did* have. This is what had been working for us all along: letting our people lead us. So we gathered a diverse group of employees representing different departments, cultures, genders, and levels of responsibility. This was a group of people we believed represented what Fetzer at its best could be. They spent a day together to identify the values by which they operate. They uncovered the following:

Respect for the land and people
Pride in quality of work
Motivated by the spirit of competition
Lead by example
Creative approach to business with a "can do" attitude
We are fun

I was blown away! I could never have come up with these values on my own, and I had no idea that these were the ones the employees felt they owned. Our context had succeeded, in just a few short years, in attracting and developing people who put the environment and respect for human beings at the top of their value list, yet who followed up immediately with exactly the values you need to succeed economically in the wine business: passion for quality and a spirit of competition. Moreover, they were up for the challenges that living out all those values would no doubt create.

Gradually it was becoming clear how we could ensure full enrollment in the purpose and make it an active part of the context and culture on a self-perpetuating basis. We would shift implementation from management to the employees. That way, they would encourage and support each other to buy into the purpose more fully, and translate it into action everywhere in the company, not just where management set up a project. The challenge was to find a way to make that shift.

AN E^3 KIND OF CULTURE

ABOUT THIS TIME, IN 1998, those of us on the Leadership Team began to hear and use the term "sustainability." The more we became familiar with it, the more it seemed to fit what we were doing. The triple-bottom-line idea was right in line with our approach. So we launched a conversation within the company about sustainability, and found that for all its richness, this term did not inspire buy-in to our purpose, and people did not see how they were supposed to put it into action. We clearly wanted to be leaders in sustainability, but the term itself was not going to get us there.

Once again, we turned to our discovery process. We got a select group of people together who were interested in environmental sustainability and played key roles in our efforts toward it. But right off, they said, "We can't look at the environment in isolation." Each knew from his or her own job that there were other costs and benefits—environmental or social or financial—of various things we were doing.

Ultimately, this Sustainability Team boiled down the aspects of the company that could not be considered in isolation: our economic bottom line, our commitment to the environment, and a desire for a more equitable world. Economics, environment, equity (for our employees and our community). Three bottom lines. Three Es. It was a short step from there to an abbreviation, E^3, that gave everyone an easy, practical shorthand for implementing our purpose.

"Sustainability" was a concept. E^3 was going to be all about action, and the Sustainability Team came up with a challenge to all the creative, can-do people at Fetzer:

We challenge ourselves to act in ways that:

benefit the people with whom we work
support the communities in which we do business
protect and sustain the environment
achieve exceptional financial returns

We had an all-hands meeting to pose this challenge under the E^3 banner, and things really took off. People looked around and saw opportunities everywhere to improve our economics, help the environment, and do more for people at Fetzer Vineyards and in the community. Almost immediately, there was no need to push projects forward from the management side. If anything, we just kept up with the flood of ideas as best we could. We would meet every six weeks with senior managers, and I didn't have to ask, "OK, what are you going to do next?" or, "OK, when are you going to show some results?" People saw their own opportunities and brought them to the meetings. Sometimes the first time we heard about some project was after it was already under way and already paying off.

That first year was amazing. There were no bad ideas, only good ones, and no shortage of people willing to run with them. Parts of the company that had been overlooked or underutilized in the past were suddenly a hotbed of initiative. Human resources was a particular example of this. Our company awards program was reborn with Green, Gold, and Platinum awards corresponding to the three Es. Our benefits plans and compensation programs got tuned up in important ways. At one meeting someone proposed a scholarship program and at the next meeting we had a whole plan for who would participate and who could apply and how much we would give and what the parameters were. Our English as a Second Language (ESL) program took off.

People started using "E^3" as shorthand for how we wanted to run our business. They would say, "Where's the E^3 in that?" or "That's a good idea—could you E^3 it up?" We knew then that it was woven into the fabric of the culture.

E^3 also changed other understandings inside the business as well. It came out one day in an E^3 discussion that some of our workers from Mexico thought our emphasis on recycling meant we were cheap—recycling Coke cans to get two cents was what people did in poor places, not a rich place like Fetzer. E^3 gave us the perfect vehicle for changing that perspective. Under E^3, recycling was not about the two cents or saving money, it was about protecting the environment for our kids. Pretty soon these same workers were coming up with E^3 ideas of their own.

In the years after E^3 got rolling, we hit new highs in revenues and earnings, had the top-selling Merlot in the country, continued to win significant industry quality awards, and built up our cooperage to meet surging demand for our premium American oak barrels. Resource conservation and environmental protection had been important before, but now they were part of a crusade. We committed ourselves to zero waste. We began restoring habitat along watersheds. We started an employee commuter van program to cut down on vehicle emissions.

We had the third annual E^3 meeting in a big warehouse at the winery in 2000. At one point, the doors opened to the warehouse and this tractor came putt-putting in. I had no idea why. It turned out the vineyard team was about to announce that they just started using bio-diesel fuel instead of petrochemical diesel in the tractors. Six months later, our facilities director, who manages the trucking department, which includes 18-wheelers that haul bottles and barrels, sent me an e-mail that said, "It's time for us to try it in our trucks." He'd stepped back and watched how bio-diesel worked in the tractors for a little while. No one was saying to him, "You have to do this in the trucks." When it was time, he knew it without anyone telling him.

We have a companywide E^3 meeting every year, to review how we did on last year's E^3 goals and set out our goals for the coming year. Everything's spoken about in the E^3 format, because increasingly, we can't say something is just economic or just environmental. Organic farming might cost more than conventional farming in some people's eyes, no matter what the environmental benefits. But soon it will be a competitive market advantage through higher grape quality, enhanced brand reputation, and greater appeal in markets such as the U.K., where people have a high value for organically grown products. These advantages all have the potential to benefit our financial results.

As the years have passed, people's ideas are getting bigger. Their expectations have definitely been raised. They want to see even bigger things happen. Once a month, someone sends me a note about alternative fuel vehicles. We're using electric cars now and exploring other options in that area. There are still no bad ideas, it's just that some of them are harder to implement than others. People want us to get off the power grid, for example, and go full solar. We are partially solar now, but powering the whole business without buying from the utilities would upset the E^3 balance from an economic standpoint. So we're looking for ways to move that balance to a better point, by using cogeneration, reducing electricity use, and keeping an eye on solar technology as it becomes more affordable. Fortunately, our culture is such that people consider it fun, creative, and competitive in a good way to do things that no other winery has ever done. So we'll keep figuring out ways to make all three Es work.

Ultimately, the best thing about all these ideas is that they're not coming out of people's job descriptions. They're growing naturally out of the culture of the company, which is determined by the new context we set for it—together.

THIRD PRINCIPLE

THE SOUL OF A BUSINESS IS FOUND IN THE HEARTS OF ITS PEOPLE

Shortly before I became president of Fetzer, I had taken a two-month management class in problem solving and teamwork. It was a fairly intense class that met every weekend over a period of two months. One weekend we were divided into small groups and given an unusual exercise: depicting a declarative statement using clay. I was surprised to learn that this interpretive exercise was designed to take most of the weekend. Obviously there was going to be no right or wrong answer, but I couldn't see how molding some clay was going to take a day and a half.

Then I saw who was in my group, and my heart sank. One of my new team members, whom I'll call Veronica, was someone I saw as pretty sharp. She was intelligent, had a solid business background, and had been active and involved in class. The other team member, Tracey, I had pegged as being needy, emotional, and scattered. I could already see in my mind how this would play out. Veronica and I were going to have to solve this problem together, with or without Tracey's contribution.

Before we could begin, we were supposed to tell each other anything that might make it difficult for us to work together as a team. Uh-oh. When it came to my turn, I couldn't tell Tracey what I thought about her. So I said something noncommittal and got it over with. I was, shall we say, less than honest.

Finally we sat down to work with the clay. But when we saw the statement we were supposed to depict—"Man's reach should exceed his grasp, or what is a heaven for?"—we didn't know how to approach it. Right away it got frustrating. Sure enough, I felt Veronica was smart and on my wavelength, and I thought she had good ideas, or at least ideas I could work with. Tracey's ideas were hopeless as far as I could see, and it took a lot of energy to work around them or negate them. An hour of frustrating work kept leading to dead ends, and it was this ditzy woman who was making it so hard, I thought. My lack of respect for her festered into active dislike. I began to understand how we could burn up the entire weekend with this exercise in futility.

Suddenly I realized I had been here before. Not only had I been here before, but I was here a lot: making snap judgments, offering others little respect, and not listening very well. I acted like I was listening to Tracey, but I was actually using whatever she said as evidence for my judgments about her. I was effectively making the exercise be about her, not the clay. It dawned on me that it was not Tracey who was preventing us from making progress. It was me.

So I consciously shifted my perspective. I told myself that Tracey was brilliant, and that anything she said was a step toward the solution. I turned my lack of respect around and willed myself to see her as my equal. Tracey would lead Veronica and me to an early completion of the exercise, and it would be the best damn clay model in the class. (I might have lost my disrespect, but I had not lost my competitiveness.)

Within an hour, we had completed the exercise.

In hindsight, I see Tracey was contributing useful ideas from the start, but I'd blocked them. By not respecting her, I had missed everything she had to offer. Once I shifted my perspective and began listening to her ideas, our team started gaining momentum right away. Not only that, Tracey did the majority of the breakthrough thinking. It was no longer necessary to will myself to respect her. She had earned it—once I was able to allow that possibility inside my own head.

One of the other teams finally finished the clay exercise well into the second day, and the third team never finished. They fought with each other to the bitter end, each one pushing his own agenda and ideas, each blocking the others' contributions, even yelling loudly at one another. It was painful for them, but a tremendous reinforcement for me.

I returned to work and began to look at my relationships differently. I had to accept the disconcerting fact that I wasn't a very good listener. I would sit and politely listen to the ideas of an employee, with my mind already made up. I would let them finish and then say, "Those are good thoughts, but I think I want you to..." As long as I was dealing solely with ideas or concepts—listening only for the logic or agreement that would be in synch with my own point of view—the people didn't actually matter that much to me. They were just a messenger, a speaker, a vehicle for an idea.

So I decided to repeat the same exercise that I was supposed to do with Tracey before we started in on the clay. I sat down my winemaking team members, one at a time, and told them the ways I had been holding them in my mind. To my chagrin, they were not surprised. They knew already that I was judging them in some way. In each case, I said I would drop the way I had been thinking of them and try to see them for who they really were. It worked. People I had judged as nice to be around but lousy contributors now had a chance to contribute and get recognized for it. People whose responsibility I had restricted for some reason now had a chance to step into new areas of personal expression.

My success in clearing away judgments with coworkers gave me confidence to try it with a much tougher crowd: my own family. My relationship with my son Jason had gotten into a pretty bad state during his teenage years, when I was just totally focused on work. When I was at home, I expected everything to fit my perspective and my needs, but Jason wasn't playing his assigned role. I saw this as disrespectful. I saw it as selfish. Above all, I saw it as his fault. He was My Son The Jerk. This became a self-fulfilling prophecy, and things just got worse between us.

After the clay exercise with Tracey, I realized the way I was holding Jason in my mind was more about me than about him. I was the one who needed to bring a little more respect to the relationship. Once I dropped my harsh interpretation of him, he was able to be the loving, caring son he truly was. We transformed our relationship and now he, his brother Heath, and I are partners in a business together.

I started to see that all my significant business and personal relationships were based to some degree on my interpretation of the individuals involved. I personally wanted to be seen for who I was but I was not offering this same respect in return. The consequence for Fetzer was far-reaching. I was holding back the entire company.

Once I began seeing people as more than just bearers of news, ideas, or suggestions, I could detect the magnitude of pride, passion, and talent within them. I began to understand what people mean when they say someone is "a great listener": that person fully respects others as special, powerful, unique, and with something important to contribute. One of the best things about being this kind of listener is that you get much more than the literal meaning of what the person is saying. You also can pick up why he's saying it, what his bigger picture looks like, and what it could signal to you about your own perspective or your own blind spots. You get a whole wealth of information that the other person may not even know he's communicating.

On my Leadership Team, I've got people in their twenties, thirties, forties, and fifties. It would be easy to assume that the older people have more to offer. Or if the topic is wine quality, it's easy to assume that I should listen to what our winemaker has to say, not what our marketing or financial people have to say. The reality is, anyone in the room could have something to offer that's new, important, and potentially a breakthrough. If someone is willing to speak up in a meeting, it's because they have seen something and believe it will make a difference. When we honor that, it alters the whole dynamic. My team can see me giving them the space to actually express their creativity.

One of the best examples of this involves Bob Blue, whom I had put in charge of our new red wine facility in Hopland. Bob had a great reputation, but I hadn't worked with him all that long. In his job, he was responsible for the crush, the fermentations, initial blending of the wines, running the facility, and managing the workers there. I had given him this authority, but I also suspected he couldn't handle it. So I was spending a lot of time at the facility, second-guessing him or telling him what I thought he should do.

When I opened up to him, Bob stepped in with more confidence. Among other things, he began expressing his interest in organic winegrowing. Within two years, he was in charge of the

Bonterra line. When Fetzer eventually spun off Bonterra in 1995 and it became a separate division of Brown-Forman, Bob took charge of the whole business. It's hard to think that I missed the chance to respect him more from the beginning.

FROM ACCOUNTABILITY TO "RESPONSE-ABILITY"

ONCE I SET ASIDE my judgments and allowed everyone at the company to contribute more fully, people seemed to follow a natural progression. They moved from being accountable for certain predefined results to taking personal responsibility for our larger mission. When I limited their contributions (either by not seeing their full capability or by simply imposing guidelines or limitations) they could be accountable, but often without enthusiasm. They could, and would, do whatever task I set them. They could fulfill their job requirements. But it was not always meaningful to them, and that meant it was not all that meaningful for the company. When I removed the limits, people could not only be accountable for delivering results, they could see their job as part of a larger challenge. They could respond to Fetzer's larger purpose with initiative and creativity of their own.

This freedom, within the context we had set and were constantly reinforcing, unleashed the power of our people. It allowed them to intuitively match their own capabilities and interests—which I might know nothing about—with opportunities they saw to contribute. They could be come "response-able," not just accountable.

The new possibility for business is to make this same shift at an organizational level. Rather than viewing accountability to our shareholders as a measure of how well we enhance shareholder value and hit financial targets, we can begin responding to the growing social and environmental challenges the world faces today. These challenges are not extraneous to business. They are, increasingly, part of the landscape in which we all must perform. Responding to social and environmental challenges so our companies can operate efficiently—investing less in contentious public policy debates that drive extreme regulations, for example—is an essential part of operating profitably. If we recognize and tackle such issues as an integral part of our new way of looking at business, we'll find equitable solutions and ultimately reduce the cost of doing business. Furthermore, every business can respond in its own way, with its own unique capabilities, making its own special contribution. Along with making profits, we can make a difference.

The word "corporation" comes from the Latin *corpus*, for body. This concept evolved so that a group of people organized as a corporation could undertake activities individual people do, such as purchasing and owning property, entering into contracts, or borrowing and lending money. What resulted were corporations with the capability of an individual, but without the intangible, internal qualities that human individuals take for granted. One of those internal qualities, intelligence, was added back in the form of management. The other major internal qualities that distinguish human beings are heart and soul, which have not always been the hallmark of great corporations over time.

Recent corporate history suggests that heart and soul are not required for a business to be accountable to shareholders. Certainly the corporations and executives involved in corporate scandals as we entered this new century seemed to think that morality was optional, even a hindrance to achieving results.

I believe that for sustainable businesses to shift from accountability to responsibility, we need to put heart and soul back into the *corpus*. A sustainable business should be a whole business, like a whole person. It must have integrity. It must have a moral center. It must be connected to its values and the greater world. It must aspire to do what is right, not just for the bottom line, not just from a legal standpoint, but from a moral and ethical standpoint. It's not only accountable, it's responsible.

The wholeness we managers seek for our business is already all around us, every day. The capacity is in our people, who are simultaneously the fabric of the company and the fabric of our world. They connect the business to the larger system automatically because they live in that system, both as workers and as consumers. They are not like corporations, legally defined without souls. They are people with lives and aspirations and families. They are the ones whose children will not have clean air and water if we don't protect the environment. They are the ones whose grandchildren will live in a world of strife and terror if we don't pay attention to human rights. If you ask them, I believe they will also tell you that they want to live in a more sustainable world.

How do we get all these qualities, of heart and soul and commitment to something greater, to show up in our people? Our experience at Fetzer led to the third principle of sustainable business leadership. *The soul of a business is found in the hearts of its people.*

IF YOU SEE YOUR PEOPLE AS GREAT...

SO WHAT CAN MANAGEMENT DO to find this kind of heart and soul everywhere in the business? While we're still discovering the answer to that question at Fetzer, some clear lessons have emerged for me. Our employees have an infinite potential to contribute. We can intentionally see each of our people as big contributors, and provide the biggest possible stage to play out that contribution. If you believe they can be great, they will be. If they don't look like your picture of greatness at first, maybe that's because of your perspective, not their potential.

When you drive past a large California vineyard at various points during the year, you're likely to see crews of workers pruning last year's vine growth, or thinning new shoots, or pulling leaves to get more air and sunlight to the grapes. It's likely that everyone you see is of Hispanic origin, and the crews at Fetzer are no different. But a large, generic label like "Hispanic" is a mask. It hides the individuality that's present in each person. At Fetzer, some of our people are immigrants from Mexico. Some were born in the United States, into families that emigrated one or two generations back. Some speak no English. For some, it's their first language. Some are single, some have families. They all have their own story, their own aspirations, their own life path—and you can't tell what it is by appearances.

Imagine an employee who has just arrived from Mexico and is just learning English, so he seems a bit shy. His reticence and our inability to speak to him in his language, combined with his economic status, make it easy to assume that he is not that well educated, not that polished. In most businesses, including the wine business, this worker would be assigned to work in the vineyards as a laborer, or as a cellar worker in a barrel room. He would be expected to literally punch the clock and deliver so many hours of labor per day.

We have learned that this perspective is not just unfair to him, it's unproductive for us. Look again. See a courageous man who has moved his entire family to a new country to create opportunity for them. He is providing for his family, making the most of his finances, and enjoys a rich community life away from the job that we never see. After work, on weekends, he helps organize a cultural association that preserves the best of his country's traditions, even as he learns the new traditions of his adopted country. He learns English, and makes sure his children take school seriously. From the proper perspective it's clear that this individual is a hardworking entrepreneur, capable of much more than punching a clock. He's not a unit of labor, he's an inspiration.

If we see our people as the heart and soul of our business, we let them shift naturally from accountability to responsibility. Here are some examples I've gathered along the way.

Kate Frey and Bridget Harrington lead our organic garden and our culinary programs, respectively. In basic terms, they are charged with developing programs and activities to showcase Fetzer Vineyards wines. Ultimately, Kate and Bridget are accountable as part of our marketing group to create connections and relationships that help sell more wine by enhancing Fetzer's image with key customers. Bridget, our chef, works closely with Kate, our gardener, to use the bounty of our garden in these efforts. Their accountability could have easily ended with wine and food education programs directed at chefs, sommeliers, and wine buyers from key retailers. They're good at these things, they understand them well, and there's plenty to do on any given work day. But our sustainable business environment within Fetzer allowed for more.

Kate and Bridget live in our community, and they're well aware of the world around them. They noticed that most people didn't know very much about nutrition, even less about organic gardening and farming. Without forming a committee, writing a report, or asking to build a new community relations department, they simply took action. Today, local schools bring eager students to Kate's five-acre organic garden at Valley Oaks, where they learn first-hand about where food comes from and the organic way of producing it. They pick vegetables, fruits, and nuts and join Bridget in our winery kitchen to prepare their own organic meal. Kate is now working with schools and teachers to help them plant their own gardens, and Bridget is involved in the local healthy lunch program for school kids. Both serve as ready resources, often investing far more of their own energy and time than I would have ever felt comfortable asking for. By taking true responsibility, Kate and Bridget connected us more strongly to the larger system of our local community, enhancing our relationship and ability to build on that relationship to achieve our goals.

I realize that most businesses don't have organic gardens and culinary programs, so I'll give you an example in a more familiar department: purchasing.

Sue Hawley is accountable for procuring packaging, which for wineries includes bottles, corks, labels, and shipping cases, along with related services such as printing. We've been growing steadily and adding new products for years, and the packaging industry has seen the same dynamics of competition, offshore production, consolidation, and technological change that are making life so interesting for businesses everywhere. So Sue can hardly do her job by rote. There's a lot to coordinate between the needs of our production and marketing teams and suppliers. And as with all purchasing, there's a lot of serious negotiating to do. Packaging can be as much as 25 percent of our cost of goods, so there's a lot of money involved and a significant net effect on our profitability.

Most businesses want their purchasing departments to grind away on reducing costs while maintaining both supply lines and quality products and services. Even at a triple-bottom-line company such as Fetzer, you might imagine that we would take the same approach. That's not exactly how Sue saw it.

When we rolled out our E^3 program, providing the context for how we wanted to run our business, Sue immediately began to think about what it meant for her. She knew she had a big influence on the economic E, and she was also able to influence the environmental E by making sure that we buy bottles and cardboard cases made with the maximum amount of post-consumer/recycled materials available. Yet Sue saw that she could expand E^3 outside of Fetzer as well, and have a positive influence on the environmental practices of our suppliers and the whole wine industry, using our vendor evaluation system.

This system was already well developed in terms of grading and comparing vendors on quality, cost, and service. Sue added an environmental component, giving vendors positive points for things like delivering our materials in reusable containers, developing environmentally friendly processes and materials, and reducing waste in their own production processes. Sue gave our vendors an incentive to view their own businesses through the lens of sustainability and compare their own environmental performance against their competitors.

I realize that some people might view this approach as imposing our values on others. My answer is, not in a free market. Suppliers don't have to do business with us, because there are hundreds of other wineries in California. In fact, we believe we're creating an opportunity for our vendors to align their own interests with ours, creating a synergy that didn't exist previously. On a purely practical plane, they have a chance to do research and development into new papers or inks with the knowledge that they have a major customer that is willing to pay for those advances. Once they have refined them, they can sell them to anyone. So if we're imposing anything, it's a positive new possibility.

In Sue Hawley's instance, her immediate influence was in her direct, accountable area of our business: buying packaging. But in our culture at Fetzer, good examples generate excitement and win followers. Today the other members of Fetzer's purchasing department follow Sue's packaging model for everything we acquire. An administrative function that many companies might view as accountable only to the economic bottom line is now helping make the world a better place environmentally and socially, one purchasing contract at a time.

SETTING LOOSE THE ENERGY OF EMPLOYEES

SEEING PEOPLE AS GREAT so they can show up as great involves more than just a shift in perception. It also involves practical issues of creating space for people to fully express their contribution once we've removed internal limits on them. A number of years ago, we noticed that our bottling teams were not as diverse as they should be. All the line workers were Hispanic, and all the supervisors and managers were Anglo. Some of the team members had been working the line for 15 or 20 years, and they knew better than anyone how it worked and what we needed to improve it. They certainly knew more than any recent college graduate we assigned as their supervisor. This was clearly unacceptable from a social equity standpoint, and it wasn't doing much to maximize our productivity either.

So we decided to bring line workers into management. We figured the best way to do this was to replace the Anglo supervisors with the line workers who had gotten along with their supervisors the best. This was a miserable failure, because—we now understand—we were still stuck in the old model, looking for someone the rest of management might have the most success in holding accountable.

We kept talking about the situation on the bottling lines and began to notice that it was similar in the cellar and on our vineyard team as well. We needed more than a supervisory change in production. We needed a new model entirely. Finally, we hit on the idea of eliminating supervisors completely. If we truly believed veteran employees knew their jobs well, what purpose did supervisors serve? We did need a way to make sure that training was conducted for new employees in an effective manner, and there are always some administrative records to be managed. We still wanted to have a smaller group with which we could share ideas and insights. So we created a new position called "team coach," one for each production team.

We invited anyone to apply, and this time we got it right. The people who stepped forward did so voluntarily, because they had ideas and wanted to implement them or because they wanted to take more responsibility on behalf of their fellow team members. They weren't always the people we expected to apply, based on things like age or seniority. They were, however, the workers their own colleagues would naturally respect, and that was the key. Productivity on the bottling lines began going up month by month. It's never been higher. We provided some training and language tutoring where necessary, but we haven't invested heavily to make up for something that was not there. When we let ourselves imagine the production teams as capable of producing their own team coaches, they did. When we saw those team coaches as capable of doing an even better job than the supervisors they replaced, they did.

This is a perspective leaders in sustainable businesses need to embrace for all their people, not just the ones coming in at the bottom of the socioeconomic ladder and working in a production facility far from the corner office. Bright, literate, highly visible workers can also be hiding immense talents.

CREATING AN ENVIRONMENT OF FULL EXPRESSION

THERE'S A MANAGEMENT THEORY that successful businesses are not due to their people—they're due to having the *right* people. According to this view, you just go out and find the best people, compensate them properly, and rake in the profits.

I believe there's more to it. I believe that if you respect the people you have for their entire potential and personality, for their total capacity for self-expression, they will *become* the right people. Even if you hire the best controller around, that person has a lot more to offer than simply an ability to control financial flows. Your job as a leader is to provide an environment for this whole expression to come out. From a leadership standpoint, you set the direction and then allow people to contribute from their own perspective, knowledge, and experience.

If anything, the so-called "right people" are most likely to be the ones who are fully aligned with the business's purpose, context, and culture. Allowed to fully express themselves, they won't ever stop growing. Soon their job descriptions will be far smaller than their actual contributions. This was certainly the case with a man named Keith Roberts, who made a major difference at Fetzer from the unlikely position of barrel repairman.

One of the major elements of quality winemaking in California is oak barrels, which we use for aging most wine and for fermenting some wines. When you hear people speak of "wood" in a wine's flavor, this is what they mean. At Fetzer Vineyards, we have more than 100,000 such oak barrels in use at any given time. Although we can use a barrel for a number of years, there's a constant need for new ones, and they're expensive, averaging several hundred dollars apiece. Part of the cost comes from the "toasting" of the insides of the barrels. This charring changes the wood in ways that make it more effective for aging wine. You can also toast the barrel more or less deeply, depending on the effect you want in the finished wine.

In 1992, our winemaking team decided to hire a barrel cooper named Keith Roberts to repair and restore barrels. The idea was simply to reduce our barrel costs and postpone the day when another tree had to be cut down for new barrels. Keith's job was to fix anything on a barrel that was broken or worn out. Then he would scrape out the old charred wood in a barrel to expose new wood, and re-toast it inside to the specifications of the winemaker. This repair and restoration effort gave us the equivalent of an expensive new oak barrel at a fraction of the cost. We called this a "double-E" project: It worked both economically and environmentally.

Everybody was happy with how this worked out, but Keith did have a question after a while. Even as he reconditioned old barrels, we continued to purchase new heads (the ends of the barrels) so that at least some part of the barrel was new wood. Keith asked why. The answer was, we were trying to find the best combination of reconditioned wood and new wood. If that was the point, he said, then why didn't we make the new heads ourselves? The money we saved would pay for us to hire a person to make them, and we would have even more control over our experiments. Keith then pointed out that some of the barrels he was repairing had to be rebuilt almost from scratch. If we had the tools and the expertise to do that, why did we have to buy barrels at all?

This was kind of an amazing question. At the time, no winery had an in-house cooperage. Not even the barrel companies were making a great American oak barrel, because no one knew anything about where the American oak wood should come from. In France, the coopers have made barrels for centuries, creating forests filled with trees that produce wood expressly for barrel staves. They have even developed forests matched to various types of wine. Nobody had worked that out in America. We know oak trees provide different characteristics depending on where they are grown, but we didn't know which trees should be grown in which areas to interact with which wine. That's why wineries all bought different barrels from a wide variety of coopers and tried to find the best combination of wood and wine. Keith's question made us realize that if the French could figure it out, so could we.

Making our own barrels was virgin territory, and Keith was ready to head into it. The winemakers were right behind him. They were experimenting, discovering, and exploring the impact of various winemaking techniques on our wines all the time. We were doing as many as 100 experiments a year, often involving wood and barrels and aging. The decision was made not because we had all the answers but because we couldn't see any reason not to let people bring forth everything they had. We would keep a close eye on costs and wine quality, of course, but how the barrel guys advanced was up to them. It was their idea, and they got to run with it.

The barrel-making operation started out producing just a few barrels a day. Now it's a full-fledged independent business, called the Mendocino Cooperage, employing 50 people and capable of making

240 barrels a day. We still get exactly the barrels we want, when we want them, and we get them for less money than we could do it any other way. No one said to Keith Roberts, "your job is to create the Mendocino Cooperage at Fetzer." We just gave him the space to keep expressing his response to the larger opportunity, and that's where it led. Other wineries now buy 80 percent of the barrels made by Mendocino Cooperage, because those wineries also want customized, high-quality American oak barrels. So Keith's original question ultimately has benefited the whole industry, along with millions of wine drinkers.

In case you're wondering if other wineries have their own cooperages now, the answer is no. The rare exceptions only prove the rule. A conventional business analysis might conclude that the reason wineries don't vertically integrate this way is because, on paper, running a cooperage is not a core competency for wine producers. How it looks on paper is not enough for us. We look at the people, and if there is a core competency in them, and they are willing and able to express it at Fetzer Vineyards, then we're willing to make space for it to become a competency for the company. Again, we keep a close eye on costs and quality, then get out of the way and let people show up as great.

Our trucking division is another good example. We certainly weren't looking to start a trucking company, but one started itself inside Fetzer and just kept growing. Keith Oakley started as a delivery driver, taking wine 120 miles down to the San Francisco Bay Area. When we expanded to a second winery in the 1980s, we needed a tanker truck to move bulk wine between locations. Keith found the right truck and began driving it.

As we kept expanding our business, we kept needing more transportation, and Keith just kept saying, "we can do that." Thanks to this can-do attitude, Fetzer quietly acquired a dozen trucks. One day we realized that this was a sizeable fleet for a winery. Everything was working well, but most of our competitors use common carriers so we thought we had better do a benchmarking analysis. It turned out Keith and his team were running a pretty tight outfit. Our cost per mile averages as much as a third below what we would pay common carriers for the same services, and we were setting standards for safety and efficiency that any outside company would find hard to maintain.

Our costs are lower because Keith and his team are totally into it. We don't give them much of a budget, but that doesn't bother them. They're truck guys. They not only like to drive the trucks, they like to work on the trucks. They like to be around them and they like to talk about them. They're fully expressing their passion for trucks, and we're giving them the space to do that. In that context, they have turned out to be truly great at what they're doing.

FULL-CYCLE ACKNOWLEDGEMENT

CERTAINLY ALL THE INDIVIDUALS I've described are exceptional in some way. The lesson, however, is not that Fetzer is full of exceptional people. I believe all businesses have an abundance of great people. The difference may be that at Fetzer, we make sure our people are working in an environment where they feel inspired to express their passion and creativity fully.

Awards and acknowledgment programs are pretty standard in corporate America, and Fetzer is no different. We have awards for our E^3 program, we have spot awards for outstanding efforts on an ad hoc basis, and we have days when we just shut down production and let people play games all day and have a barbecue party for lunch. Other businesses have their own versions of these. But I have noticed an interesting twist on acknowledgement that may be useful to other businesses as well.

Imagine a manager down the hall who does a great job, both accountable to specific results and responsible to the larger mission. Everything's great, except that he comes in around 9:30 in the morning, not 8:00 or 8:30 A.M. like you do. He reports to you, but he's coming in an hour and a half after you. I used to see such a person as flawed, not great. I would see him as missing an obvious opportunity to impress his boss and his team. I would see this failure every time I passed his office, every time I talked with him in the hall, every time I saw his car pull into the parking lot. It would simply tick me off.

The hidden consequence of this perspective is that I can no longer acknowledge this person's positive contribution in my own mind. How am I going to see him as great and give him a chance to fully contribute? I can't. So I've given up one of the best ways a manager has to motivate and reward people.

But that's not all I've done. If you think about it, I have also limited my own ability to contribute to this person, and that is counter to my whole mission. Addressing people's deficits always works best in concert with acknowledging their successes and strengths, but now I can't do that. I'm stuck on the deficit. So what's the solution? I have to shift my perspective, see what he has to offer, and acknowledge the heck out of that. This is not a freebie for him. Once I can acknowledge what's good or great about him, I then have a basis—not to mention a relationship with him—that enables me to start contributing more to him. I can talk with him about what else I'd like to see, not the one thing that's bugging me.

People come in complicated packages. You have to leave your options open as far as acknowledging people. Respect them beforehand for how they express their individual human spirit. Acknowledge their accountability even before they respond to the larger opportunity, and acknowledge them publicly when they make the shift to responsibility. Such feedback creates a new future for people, because how others see them, and how they see themselves, is different. They're clearer than ever about what works for them and for everyone. Ideas or actions they might have held back before—or that might never have occurred to them—are now that much closer to benefiting the business in tangible ways. And that creates a new future for the company.

Ultimately, this is one of the most sustainable cycles in human progress: being respected for our ability to make a contribution, being given opportunities to express that ability fully, and being acknowledged for it afterward. This is the inner psychological engine that drives most of us to personal achievement—that gets us to put our heart and soul into something.

In a sustainable business, it should be no different.

FOURTH PRINCIPLE

TRUE POWER IS LIVING WHAT YOU KNOW

One late winter morning in 2000 my phone rang. It was a call I'll never forget.

That day spring was already beginning to show, with big, puffy white clouds in a brilliant blue sky above the dark green hills to the southwest. Just outside my office window, the cover crops between the vine rows were starting to wake as the days began to warm. It was a beautiful scene, and I was in a pretty good mood.

Fetzer Vineyards had just closed on an historic old farm called the Butler Ranch, and I was thinking about the wines we could make from the new vineyard we would plant there. The ranch is on a high ridge not far from the winery. The Butler family had a pretty big orchard up there, mostly cherries. As time went by, they had converted the orchard to a pick-it-yourself, have-a-lot-of-family-fun operation, a change that was received enthusiastically by the Mendocino community. Every year, families would flock to the mountain, navigating the twisting, poorly maintained roads to spend the day picking fruit and picnicking, creating memories that crossed generations. The views were breathtaking, the cherries always the sweetest, and families planned special days each year.

Over time, however, the property fell into disrepair. Disease had attacked the trees, and the fences were rotting. The ponds had breached, the roads were washing out, and erosion was rampant. Eventually the Butlers decided to sell, and Fetzer was fortunate enough to buy it. We had to compete against another bidder, and I believe that what swung the deal our way was my vision of farming the ranch using organic farming techniques.

We had been moving ahead on an overall development plan for the ranch. Roads had to be improved, and we needed to rebuild fences, recondition the ponds, find a consistent supply of water, and reengineer the slopes to prevent further erosion problems. We would also need to remove most of the cherry trees to make room for new vineyard. All of this had to be done before we could plant a single grapevine.

Cutting down the cherry trees sounds somewhat drastic, but we didn't see it that way. One of the oldest processes in farming is replacing one crop with another, either because you need to renew the soil or because times change and you can't make a living with the old crop. Many orchards have become vineyards over time, and this would be part of that same slow evolution of agriculture in America. It's not like the trees would go to waste, either. A local woodworker had already agreed to take the cherry wood to create handcrafted furniture, so those trees would continue to serve a purpose and provide pleasure in someone's office or living room.

My head was full of these plans and the excitement that comes at the beginning of any new project, when the phone rang. It was not the woodworker, or any of the people involved in converting the ranch to vineyards. It was someone I didn't know, a community member who wanted to know if it was true that we were going to fell the cherry trees. I didn't know how he had heard this, but news travels fast in rural communities.

I talked to the man for a little while, but he did not want to hear about our vision. He wanted me to promise not to cut down any cherry trees. I told him I couldn't make a promise like that. He became insistent, then demanding. At a certain point he said something like, "You can't cut them down because we'll stop you from cutting them down!" The moment I heard that threat, I responded without thinking. "It's too late," I snapped. "They're on the ground already. We're just waiting to haul them out."

That ended this particular call, but it also started a crisis inside me. We had not cut down any trees. I had lied to the man who called me. By extension, I had lied to the whole community.

I walked the halls, wondering how this had happened. Ultimately, someone I trusted sat me down, heard me out, and helped me see that I had the power to resolve the situation. I couldn't ignore what had happened and hope it would simply go away. I had to call the man back and tell him the truth. It was hard to make my fingers dial the number, but I did it. As soon as I apologized a weight was lifted from my shoulders. The mood changed on the other end of the line, too. We talked some more, and as we talked I began to understand how important this land was. People really felt it belonged to the community. Fetzer could buy the land, but we could not buy the community's emotional stake in the property. That was not for sale.

This was an interesting new view of our larger system, and it didn't matter whether or not I liked it. It was the way it was. I eventually agreed to hold a pair of public meetings to explain to the community about the future of Butler Ranch.

The first took place a few weeks later, at our Valley Oaks Food & Wine Center. There was a lot of dialogue, with good questions and clear confirmation of what the man on the phone had told me: The community considered Butler Ranch a shared resource. As the audience members continued to speak, the reasons for these feelings became clear. The Butlers were generous and kindhearted. When local residents could not afford to pay for the cherries they picked, George Butler would not charge them. This source of free fruit, people said, was important in one of California's poorest counties, where many had low incomes and limited access to fresh produce.

I had a moment of concern at that point—my vineyard project was becoming a matter of public health!—but on the whole people were respectful when we talked about our organic farming and our triple-bottom-line approach to business. A few people expressed surprise and gratitude that a business our size had the values we demonstrated. We agreed to consider the issues that people had raised and respond after we had our second public meeting.

That meeting took place in the village of Mendocino, out on the Pacific coast. Mendocino is a large county, with a long, rugged coastline and numerous inland valleys separated by ranges of steep hills and low mountains. Despite the long distances involved, many people from the coastal areas of the county had been picking cherries at Butler Ranch for years, so we wanted to make sure we went out there to tell them about our plans.

A couple of us from the winery arrived early, set up coffee and cookies. We set up a screen and a projector in order to do a presentation about Fetzer. I stood at the entrance, meeting and greeting folks as they arrived. People were still coming in a few minutes after our scheduled start, so I waited by the door. Suddenly I heard a loud voice behind me, from the front of the room.

I turned around to hear a woman announce that the people had not come to listen to our propaganda and lies, and that they would under no circumstances lose *their* cherry orchard, and that the meeting was *theirs*.

I stood speechless as she began to make demands and threats. After a moment of disbelief, anger kicked in and my attitude hardened. I was heading for the computer, to unplug it and pack up, when something stopped me. I couldn't just hang up on this woman. A roomful of people had showed up, and storming out would not look very good. Even if I did, it was not going to end the matter.

Somehow, before I reached the computer, I remembered that when people are in your face, for better or worse, there's only one thing that works every time: Listen with respect. I told myself that these were people from my own community. Had the issue been different, I could have been in their shoes.

As others started to talk, equally upset, I moved to the front of the room and caught the eye of my Fetzer colleague. She immediately set up a flipchart and started taking notes. We started asking questions rather than just taking heat. After ten minutes that seemed like forever, the crowd started to calm down. They still insisted on telling us what was important to them, and mostly we just listened, but the tension level was dropping. Eventually I asked for some floor time to respond when they were finished. They agreed.

When it came time for me to speak, they had already seen us listen for more than an hour. They heard us repeat back and write down their concerns. Their enemy had become human again. I was not some evil developer, but a local farmer and member of the community who had somehow missed an important sentiment. I spoke honestly about how we operated as a business, and my concern for the needs of the community. I also talked about what our intentions were for the property, and they listened, mostly. In the end, the meeting went far better than I could have hoped for, considering the way it started.

These meetings were followed by several more with a self-appointed committee of folks from the coast. What we perceived were basically three types of individuals. Some simply wanted to preserve something of the contribution that the Butlers had made to the community. Others wanted their cherry orchard back. A third group just wanted a fight.

Meanwhile, there was a struggle going on inside me, too. Fetzer had purchased a beautiful piece of land. We bought it from a man who no longer wanted to be a farmer. He wanted to sell his property and retire—the Butler cherry orchard was his father's dream, not his. We wanted to create world-class wine that would win us equal recognition for our wine's quality and its environmentally sound origins. We believed the Butler Ranch would give us a great opportunity to make that kind of wine, and help us alter the course of viticulture and agriculture all over the world.

Nonetheless our purpose, no matter how important to the environmental aspect of sustainability, came at the expense of another aspect of sustainability, which is living in harmony as a positive, contributing member of our community. Putting a vineyard on Butler Ranch meant that there would not be enough trees left for a working cherry orchard, and letting people enter a working vineyard for picnics was dangerous and carried so much liability that we could not afford to risk it.

Clearing the cherry trees was a painful decision to have to make. To honor the contribution of the family to the community, we commissioned a large, colorful quilt to commemorate the Butlers and the ranch, and it made regular appearances at community events before it found a home at our offices, where it serves as a regular reminder of how we need to view our place in the larger system of our community. To continue the Butlers' tradition of generosity, we committed to support local groups dealing with community hunger and nutrition issues.

Yet that is not the end of the story. The economics at Butler Ranch didn't work if we restricted our new vineyard to the original area covered with cherry trees, so we had to expand into virgin woodlands. When we cut the indigenous trees to clear the land for vineyards, the word got out among the employees at the winery, and they were not happy about it. They understood the need to exchange a group of aging cherry trees for healthy new vines, but cutting down native oaks, madrones, and redwoods was different. Our people were not in favor of this and they let me know it. In their view, this was not an expression of E^3. It did not enhance the quality of life. Maybe it made financial sense, but we had created a context where economics don't operate in isolation from social equity. They were busting me on my own context, the one I had set for them.

And I had to admit they were right.

This whole episode, of buying and battling over the development of Butler Ranch, dramatically changed my knowledge of Fetzer's relationship to the larger system. It changed what I knew of the company's commitment to its purpose, context, and culture. I had believed I was doing what was best for our industry, and for my company's larger purpose. I believed I was living in synch with my values and the values of those around me.

The community outcry and the heartfelt sentiments from my employees created a strong sense of internal conflict for me. I wanted to get back to a sense of personal and corporate integrity. To do that, I had to adjust either my stance on land development or my knowledge about how it affected the communities we lived in.

Today, our policy is that we will not develop pristine natural landscapes into vineyards. We'll convert agricultural land, but we'll never again harvest a forest for a vineyard. This doesn't change what happened at Butler Ranch, but it is a living, lasting legacy. It places our future actions back in alignment with what we believe.

The lesson I took away from this story is the fourth principle of sustainable leadership: *True power is living what you know.*

INDIVIDUAL INTEGRITY, BUSINESS INTEGRITY

WE HEAR, as individuals, about global warming and its potential to scorch the earth. We hear about hunger and famine in supposedly developed countries. We hear about a frightening acceleration in species extinction. We hear about rising rates of cancer from environmental causes. We hear all this, and if we're honest, we know that humanity has had a hand in it, however unintentional. We know that a narrow focus on unchecked economic growth and development by the wealthiest nations, without effective regard for other societies, other species, or the environment cannot last forever. Something has to change.

Now consider that our businesses are extensions of ourselves. Business operates in a world that is becoming unstable both politically and socially, and increasingly exhausted environmentally. To do nothing is to deny our values as individuals.

We've seen that the legal separation of a corporation from its workers does not exempt the workers from the consequences of the corporation. Companies such as Enron can go bankrupt and even disappear, but the people at Enron who lost their retirement accounts did not disappear. Those people are still here, and they've got a much less attractive future ahead of them. If our businesses bankrupt our environmental and social future, we as individuals are left holding the bag in the same way. But in simply living what we know to be true, we have the power to change history.

INEVITABLE ACTION

ONE MORNING IN 1986, Jim Fetzer, then president of Fetzer Vineyards, and I were standing in the winery's new organic garden, marveling at the incredible colors and flavors all around us. The garden came from Jim's realization that food is the natural setting for wine. Wine and food naturally go together. This seems obvious now, but back then no winery had made that connection as a part of their product presentation. So Jim hired Michael Maltas (*Organic Gardening* magazine named him its organic gardener of the year in 1985) to put in a garden that would bring people up to the winery and help us showcase our wines in the context of enjoying fine food. To Jim, the organic angle was an extra hook because the focus was on wine as an essential part of a healthy, positive lifestyle.

Michael did not see it that way. He was living what he knew, and if wine was to be part of that, well, fine. What he knew was organic farming. As Jim and I were standing there, tasting fruits and vegetables and having a transcendent gastronomic moment, Michael came up to us with challenge written all over his face. "Look," he demanded, "how can you expect me to farm this way, when you guys are spraying chemicals in the vineyards? How can I be true to what I am trying to express here if there's poison all around?"

With the garden's amazing tastes bursting in our mouths and Michael's words ringing in our ears, Jim and I just looked at each other. He was right. We had to try growing grapes the same way. That was the beginning of organic viticulture at Fetzer. We started experimenting in the vineyards that year. The fruit was so much more flavorful that we were launched solidly on a totally new path.

I have looked back at that seminal moment many times. Michael had created a perfectly balanced mini-ecosystem that attracted the right combination of beneficial insects and pollinators. In just two years, there were a thousand different varieties of fruits, vegetables, herbs, and edible flowers to enjoy. He knew how to do all that. But he knew something more, and he could not ignore it any longer. He knew that his garden was part of a larger system, and that the chemicals we were putting into the soil and water were going to affect his garden. They were going to undercut all his hard work—the work we had hired him to do. Once he knew that, he had to act from that knowledge even if it meant confronting his boss. The power his integrity gave him changed history at Fetzer, and the results are still unfolding today.

I now see that everyone, and every business, can act as Michael Maltas did. We can stop ignoring what we know to be vital truths. We can confront the conventional way of doing things. We can stop ignoring the unavoidable reality that we are operating unsustainably, as businesses and as a culture. We can demonstrate a new possibility for business, by shifting to sustainable practices. And we can help others pursue new possibilities in their own businesses. If we don't do this, we are violating our own integrity.

If I lack integrity, it's because I'm not acting from what I know to be my own values. I'm not whole, I'm divided against myself. If a corporation lacks integrity, it's because the corporation is acting from some of its values, but against others. It's expressing the value of its stakeholders in seeking to maximize shareholder value, but suppressing the values of its stakeholders who respect the environment and human rights. In contrast, removing that internal conflict unleashes tremendous creative power. It encourages people to really express what they believe, because the whole organization believes it, too.

INTEGRITY-BASED BUSINESS BRINGS BOLD CHALLENGES

PEOPLE ASK ME all the time, how do you do what you're doing as a subsidiary of a larger, publicly traded company? We would love to do that, they say, but our corporate parents would never let us.

My answer is always the same: Brown-Forman not only lets us, it encourages us. We would not be Fetzer if we were not living what we know to be true about our world and our ability to make a difference in it. What would Brown-Forman own if we were not doing that? It would own some manufacturing facilities and some agricultural contracts. That's not what it wants. It wants a fully integrated company, with values that fit its own values. For us, maximizing profits is not separable from a larger mission, it's a part of it, and Brown-Forman sees that. It's living what it knows by owning us.

Having this kind of integrity-based business can bring up some interesting and unique challenges. Right now the wine business is at the bottom of an industrial cycle that fluctuates between periods when demand outstrips supply and periods when supply exceeds demand. A huge number of new vineyard acres were planted when supply was short, and now all that production is coming on line.

Wine is backed up in distribution, because growth in consumer demand is running behind the supply. Things will balance out eventually, but at the moment there's pressure on profit margins throughout the industry, and we're not immune. We need to restore our margins quickly, and one of the few ways we have to improve them in a hurry is to bring down our grape costs.

Given our values, I would prefer to reduce our grape costs in some other way than just cutting off contracts with the growers we've cultivated over the years. I would prefer to stay in business with the growers and buy their grapes for less money rather than just end the relationship. But if I don't reduce my costs, I'm not performing in integrity with the values that Fetzer and Brown-Forman share regarding profitability. If I don't reduce my costs in a responsible and sustainable way, then I'm not performing in integrity with the values I share with my surrounding community and grower partners. I can't just forget what I know when the going gets tough. I learned that only too well from the Butler Ranch experience.

CREATE NEW KNOWLEDGE

AT FETZER, we've discovered several important facets of living what we know. One is that living out our knowledge as fully as we can generates new knowledge.

This is exactly what happened after Michael Maltas confronted Jim Fetzer and me. When we decided to grow grapes organically, all we knew was that if the food in the garden could taste that much better from organic farming, our grapes and wine might too. That was the sum of our knowledge, but living it out powered a whole process of exploration and discovery. Growing fruits and vegetables without chemicals in a garden was one thing. But when it came to growing organic wine grapes in a vineyard, we were on our own.

Michael started us in the right direction. "If you have good rich healthy soil and our great Mediterranean climate, you'll produce great flavors and quality every time," he said. We had never thought of our soil in that way. If we thought about dirt, it was how to eliminate the weeds that grew in it. So now we knew something more. The quality of the grapes depended on the quality and vitality of the soil. We went with that thought, and started working on creating organic fertilizer, and lots of it.

Setting aside a huge area for compost, we dumped all of the skins, seeds and stems from harvest, mixed them with local manure, and turned the mixture over and over throughout the year. Meanwhile, we measured the amount of organic matter in the vineyard soil so we would know how much we had to put back. We found that it takes a lot of compost—and patience—to make a difference. But we also knew, from tasting the grapes, that the fruit quality was higher. And time is a precious gift we have with every growing season.

This was the first of many times that we have come to what you might call an E^3 moment: We know that doing something costs more initially, and we also know it's better for Fetzer or our consumers or our world. So we look for a new balance among profitability, community, and the environment. As long as we stay open to exploring and discovering what E^3 harmony means right now, today, in this moment, we find ways to keep advancing. Somehow we always manage to make the economics balance with the environmental and social benefits. We needed to find a more cost-effective way to increase the organic matter in the soil than by just using compost. That led us to grow cover crops, different varieties of low-growing plants that occupy the rows between the vines. We found that if we grew big healthy cover crops, like bell beans or mustards or radishes, we could till that material into the soil and it would become what we called "green manure." It takes a little longer for the soil to break it down, but it works just fine.

We were also realizing that it was not just the soil we were working with. A vineyard is a whole ecosystem. When it is healthy and balanced, the wisdom of nature becomes obvious. Insects not only pollinate the plants and prey on the bad insects, they attract birds, which also eat the bad insects and keep down the rodent population. We found that by planting not one but two cover crops during the growing season, one in the spring and then another in the summer, we could carry the bloom sets well into September and extend the time when the insects come to the vineyard. We also learned to mow the cover crops at different times.

THE BIRTH OF BONTERRA

LEARNING THE ART of growing grapes organically took years and a lot of trial and error. Not only was it the right thing to do for the environment, for the community, and for our employees, it allowed us to make a better product. Once we knew that, we had no real choice but to convert all of our vineyards to this kind of farming. So we did.

And yet that was still not a full extension of what we knew.

Like most big wineries, we supplement our own vineyards with grapes we buy from independent growers. In fact, the majority of the fruit that goes into Fetzer wines comes from our grower partners throughout Northern California. We knew that if we could grow grapes organically, our growers could, too. We were so convinced that this was the right thing to do, we were willing to try anything, including guilt. "You know pesticides are bad," we would say. "If you farm organically, you'll be creating a healthier future for your children and their children."

It was true, of course, but they didn't know what we knew—that organic farming was successful and it would enhance the quality of our wines. They knew what their economics were, and what the market for their grapes was. Increasing their costs increased their risk. This offset any benefits of organic farming in their minds. So we changed their knowledge. We offered an initial premium of $200 per acre for organically grown grapes to help them make the shift to organics. Now they knew that in addition to helping the environment, they were helping their business. Higher risk carried higher reward.

Once we had the grapes in 1990, the question shifted to the wine. Could we produce a wine that reflected the quality and character of these delicious new organically grown grapes? And would it give us a point of difference from other wines on the market? At the time, there were more than 700 different Chardonnays in the stores. We wanted to create a Chardonnay that truly stood apart, not to win awards from wine critics (although we never mind that) but because of an authentic distinction in quality and commitment to the environment. We also wanted to give our growers a destination for all the great organic grapes they were now supplying to us.

Starting a new line of Fetzer wines was something we had done many times before. While the winemakers worked to develop and blend the wines, we began pushing on other fronts. We came up with a name for our new line of wines: Bonterra, derived loosely from Italian words for "good earth." Our marketing team designed a beautiful package, including a label with gold foil and earthen colors. It looked great, and we loved it.

But we couldn't use it.

The inks, the paper, the gold foil process—all of them were expressions of conventional, environmentally unfriendly processes. Suddenly, our marketing and procurement teams had a new mission. They found a tree-free form of paper called Kenaf to use for the labels. All the labels were printed with soy-based inks, and the cases were made from recycled corrugated cardboard. When the purchasing people found out that corks, which we buy from Portugal, are usually sanitized in a chlorine wash, they asked for corks cleaned with a process that did not involve harmful chemicals. It didn't matter that those harmful chemicals were processed in another country thousands of miles away; if they were going to be used anywhere, it was not okay. At the time, recycled bottles were financially prohibitive, but our procurement people started a dialogue with our suppliers that, even today, keeps leading to better economics in recycled glass.

The point of this whole story is that when living what we know empowers us, it unleashes new possibilities. Once we know about those possibilities, we can live in integrity with them. That in turn leads to yet more possibilities in new areas. It's a never-ending virtuous cycle of knowledge and empowerment.

LIVING WHAT YOU KNOW EXPANDS THE POSSIBILITIES

YOU CAN KICK OFF the cycle yourself, by asking one simple question: "What else could we do?" Our whole zero-waste program arose from asking this question. So did our green-power program, our elimination of chlorine and aerosols, our conversion to bio-diesel fuels, and our use of hybrid-fuel vehicles. The state of California already considers Fetzer a zero-waste business, but we're going for the real thing: Absolutely no waste by 2009.

It started with recycling: What can we stop sending to landfills and turn back into a resource? Once we knew how much could be recycled, we started seeing everything as something that should be recycled. In the vineyard, things that we had thought of as by-products, including grape skins and vine cuttings, are now valuable resources for compost. So are food waste and paper. The list of changes we made is endless, and today we're still asking what's next in this area, and the answer might surprise you. We're not looking to do more recycling, we want to do less. We want to stop bringing in material that has to be recycled. We want to contribute to the zero-waste process further upstream, by changing what and how we buy.

We made a similar shift regarding energy usage. We had taken many steps to reduce energy consumption, and we were bringing in much less energy from outside than ever before. Then we asked, "What else can we do?" The answer that came up was, we could contribute to the energy sustainability process further upstream, by buying energy from renewable sources. We could draw our power from the sun and wind, not from diminishing resources such as oil or coal or gas. That way we would be helping to make a difference even if we could not find a single additional way to reduce our consumption.

We searched out green-power providers that served California, and found it cost more than grid power. Because there is not yet a big demand for green power, it is produced in small volumes and comes to market at a slightly higher price than conventional energy.

This was not a deterrent to us, because we knew we could find an E^3 balance that made it work. In the end, we offset the higher cost by finding more efficient motors, insulating our facilities better, and reconfiguring our utility grid to be more efficient.

There is a key lesson in this example for leaders of sustainable businesses. We had already done a lot to reduce our energy consumption—and yet there was still much more we could do. Not only that, all the additional energy reduction possibilities we found had been there all along, waiting for us to discover them. We did not have to invent new technologies, we simply had to find them. We did not have to change our production processes, we simply had to enhance them. Living what we knew gave us the power to find and implement better solutions than the ones we had.

THINK SMALL, THINK BIG

WHEN I SPEAK to groups about sustainability, one of the questions I often get is, "Where do we start?" I always suggest that businesses start with the low-hanging fruit. Think of any area of the business where you know things could be more sustainable—any area where you have even the dimmest sense that there is already something you could be doing—and do it. Just take that step. The solutions are out there. They're waiting for you. Find one or two, and get the virtuous cycle going.

Of course, you don't have to start small. You can kick-start the cycle with something really big. When we began the design and construction of a new administration building in 1994, we had our construction team choose an architect, electrical engineers, mechanical engineers—everyone they needed to create this large new structure. They were all sitting together in a conference room, and I walked in and issued a challenge: "I want a building that does not deplete natural resources, either in its construction or its operation. And by the way, I don't want to pay a penny more than we would for a conventional building."

None of these people, including our own construction team, had any experience in creating a building that did not deplete natural resources. They weren't sure they knew what it meant, let alone how to do it, but they knew they could figure it out. They researched and toured, used trial-and-error and expert advice, until they came up with all the solutions, put them all together, and built an environmentally friendly building we could all be proud of. It's both modern enough and attractive enough to have won architectural awards. And it cost the same as a conventional building. The main construction material is rammed earth, quarried right from the winery grounds. It needs no further insulation. There are solar panels on the roof for energy, and the design of the building maximizes available light and natural cooling during the evening. The wood was reused from existing structures, including defunct water tanks in northern California. The rafters used to be part of a dismantled bridge from the Midwest, and the ceiling is finished with retired staves from a beer tank. We salvaged some beautiful oak doors from a condemned San Francisco office building. The paint is 100 percent recycled. We bought and refurbished recycled Herman Miller furniture. The list goes on and on.

I don't want to imply that it was all smooth sailing on this project. We had to adjust our expectations and adapt our ideas constantly. The construction team had times of extreme frustration. I can remember a pointed discussion about all the old iron nails in the recycled wood beams, which were breaking the builders' blades and splitting the wood. But they kept at it, because their frustration was outweighed by their creativity. If they had to make external adjustments in their tools or construction processes, fine. Their interior integrity stayed intact.

In fact, sometimes the only knowledge our people had in a particular area was that the status quo offended their integrity. Once, at a meeting, the cellarmaster said "We eliminated chlorine as a sanitizer in the winery." Whoever was leading the meeting said, "Great," and moved on to the next thing. I knew from my years as a winemaker that chlorine is used by wineries world-wide, despite what we know about its destructive effect on the ecosystem. Getting rid of chlorine would be both a real challenge and a great thing to share with the whole industry. So I said, "Wait a minute, how'd you do that?" The cellarmaster said, "Well, we decided to stop buying it." That was it. The cellar team had decided that what they knew about the bad effects of chlorine outweighed the fact that they didn't have a good alternative. They were going to get rid of chlorine no matter what, because that was what their integrity required.

We still have to justify such decisions economically, however, so I had a few more questions. The best alternative to chlorine appeared to be using a high-pressure spray washer. Washing out a winery as large as Fetzer Vineyards, however, would be like painting the Golden Gate Bridge. By the time you finish, you have to start over again. Did this mean we would have to hire a new worker to operate the washer full time? That would be expensive, and upset the E^3 balance in the cellar. The cellar team understood this, and ultimately they figured out how to rotate people differently so they could wash out the winery without chlorine and without hiring a new worker. Once again, this was a solution that was there all the time.

GIVE WHAT YOU KNOW

ANOTHER FACET of this principle, one that is particularly important for leaders in sustainable business practices, is that living what you know means giving what you know.

If you hold on to the knowledge you have, so that no one else can have it, then you can't go farther than you alone can go. You're stuck with what you have. Maybe no one else is getting it, but you're not getting anything more out of it, either. If you want to change the world, if you want others to do what you think should be done—everywhere, all the time—then you have to give them the means to do it. You have to give them what you know, no matter how hard you worked to get it.

At the WineVision summit meeting, our industry representatives decided that the wine industry should lead in terms of sustainable business. Once the word got out that sustainability was in, wineries that were trying things like cover crops for the first time would get their public relations people to put out stories about it. Or some winery with 10,000 acres would certify 50 acres as organic and make a big thing about it. And they got plenty of attention for it.

No winery in the country has more organic acres under ownership and management than we do, so I would angrily think, "They got all that recognition for 50 lousy acres?" Here we had certified more than 2,000 acres, created all these eco-friendly programs inside the winery, made all this progress toward sustainability, and others were getting press for just asserting that they *wanted* to be sustainable. It upset me.

Then I realized that it had nothing to do with me. Or with Fetzer. It had to do with our influence, and with what we actually were doing to change the conversation in the whole industry. We wanted to lead by example, because we're motivated by the spirit of competition. We want others to follow the best model there is—and we want that to be us!

I let go of wanting to make everyone else go through the hard work we had gone through, so they would see how much we had done and understand how far ahead we were. It might give me some personal pleasure to be acknowledged completely by everyone that Fetzer was farthest ahead, but that was not going to change the world. My pride was not as important as the larger system. I had to go the opposite way. I had to give our learning away.

I began to speak about our discoveries, and share the great results we were getting by growing without chemicals. I started getting inquiries from other growers, from other wineries in California, then from all over the country. Before long, we were getting calls from all over the world. We've had vintners from Chile, Australia, Italy, and France come to our winery to learn about the techniques for growing grapes organically, and we've been featured in *Time, Newsweek,* and on CNN. We've gained some of that recognition I saw others receiving.

When you give away what you have, you get two good things in return. First, you've made a contribution to your industry that advances your own mission. Second, you've freed yourself up to live your values and do a whole lot more that expresses your own vision. If you have given away what made you a leader, but you're still determined to enhance the quality of life and you're motivated by the spirit of competition, then you have to get back out there and do something new. You have to reconnect with your leadership instincts and find something that no one else is doing. Asking what else we can do never, ever stops.

When you do get to the point of giving away what you know, you have to be prepared that some people—maybe most people—

won't be ready to receive it yet. In 1993, six years before the Wine Vision summit, I sent a letter to the 700 other wineries then in California. I had been president of Fetzer for only one year. One of the main points I made was that the wine industry could take a stand against toxic chemicals in agriculture and become a leader in preserving the environment through our farming practices. I figured that everybody could apply what we had already learned at Fetzer, so it would not be that hard. Our industry would clean up its act, and that would be a model for all the other crops in California, the country, the world. The sky was the limit. I was really looking forward to kicking off this big, earth-changing conversation.

Except no one else wanted to have it.

A couple of tiny wineries responded and said, "Great, let's eliminate toxics! What do we do?" Two of the most eminent winery owners in the country also wrote back, but responded, "Why would we ever want to suggest that we're not an environmentally sound industry?" They just could not imagine why we would want to touch the subject. In their view, it totally upset the carefully crafted picture they were presenting to the world, of glowing sunsets seen through a glass of Chardonnay. So while I was living what I knew, so were they. What we knew was just really far apart. I was naïve about that.

Now, ten years later, it's a conversation the industry wants to have. Writing that letter challenging the industry to step forward on environmental issues helped me become a person who could play a role in this shift today. It helped me see myself as part of the industry, someone capable of addressing 700 wineries on important topics. When the Wine Vision meeting took place a few years ago, I knew enough to stand up in front of the top executives in the wine business and say, this is where I see us going. My own winery was going there, no matter what the rest of them thought. It wasn't a matter of opinion any more. It was a fact, and saying so to the leaders of my industry was no longer scary or audacious.

THE POWER OF CONVERSATION

THE ONE FINAL ASPECT of applying this principle is so simple that it's easy to overlook. But it has the power to advance you on the path of sustainability like few other actions you can take.

Think for a moment about the topics people in your company talk about most. They are likely to include products, sales growth, cost of goods, margins, and brand rankings. These are things that make up the larger conversation about maximizing profits that all businesses participate in. It's one of the most well-developed conversations on Earth. Every business has to talk about maximizing profits in order to achieve its earnings targets. There are endless conferences organized to advance this conversation, a constant stream of books about it, and ongoing academic interest in its nuances. The reason this conversation is so well developed comes from human nature. People do what they talk about, and they talk about what they do.

The corollary for sustainable businesses is that we need to talk about sustainability right along with talking about maximizing profits.

This sounds simple, but it may be one of the most radical suggestions in this book. The new possibility for business is to insert a conversation about sustainability into the conversation about maxmizing profits—and keep it there until they become the same conversation. This is the essence of the triple-bottom-line concept: talking about the environment and social equity at the same time and with the same level of commitment as we talk about maximizing profits.

HOW CONVERSATION WORKS

IN SOME WAYS, a good conversation is like a good meeting: it has the right group of participants, a strong context, and a clear focus. But that is where all similarities end.

The conversation about sustainability needs to take place everywhere: in the boardroom, on the factory floor, in sales meetings, in investor presentations. It has to be able to break out anywhere, anytime. Everyone is invited to join in at any time, and everyone can contribute. There is no agenda, just an emphasis on exploration and discovery. It's vital to sustainable businesses, because there is no road map or instruction manual. Conversation is one of the few processes on Earth that is almost guaranteed to produce new insights, new ideas, and new connections. Ideas show up between us that might never show up in our own ruminations. And because we helped create them, we can start talking about them and living what we know immediately.

Leaders have a particular role to play here—primarily in generating the conversation. It is easier for people to join almost anything in life that's already ongoing than it is to start something from scratch. If I want everyone in my organization to talk about sustainability, I need to get it rolling so they can simply join in, not have to create it themselves. That's a leader's responsibility. If you want to keep people focused on a topic, start them talking about it and keep supplying new topics and new opportunities to push for new ideas and insights.

The first retreat I organized at Leonard Lake, to find Fetzer's purpose, was really about generating conversation. I already knew I wanted to make a difference through business. I needed to get all the other key players talking about it. I needed to hear what they thought. They needed to hear what I thought, particularly as I headed into unfamiliar territory. If we listened to each other—the other essential part of conversation—then something new could develop.

After we came back from Leonard Lake, I held monthly meetings with the Leadership Team to discuss how we were going to manage the business to achieve our purpose. One of the main things we talked about was how to generate a conversation about this concept among everyone else in the company. The mission statement was one thing we used, because it was more concrete for people than "enhancing the quality of life." We got even more detailed by breaking down the areas where we felt we could make a difference and making sure we were talking about all of them:

- **People** had to be a priority, because otherwise there would be no one to enhance the quality of life, and no one to receive the benefits from succeeding at it.
- **Profit** had to be part of our context, otherwise none of us would have jobs and a vehicle for enhancing the quality of life. Our joke at the winery is, "No margin, no mission."
- **Quality** had to be part of enhancing the quality of life, because as we say in the wine business, "life's too short to drink bad wine." Bad wine would put an end to profits, pronto.
- **Consumers** were a big topic, because when you produce millions of cases of wine, you need to enhance the lives of millions of consumers.
- **Alliances** are critical to enhancing the quality of life, because U.S. law requires a three-tier system for wholesaling and retailing wine. Not only that, we also source 80 percent or more of our wine grapes from independent growers. We need to keep some rich conversations going with a broad array of strategic partners whose performances are essential to our success.

- **Our environment** is so central to our way of life that it makes no sense to think about enhancing the quality of life without taking environmental impacts into consideration. No matter what else we might be doing, we are committed stewards of the land that we live on.
- **The community** we are a part of was also a topic. Where and how we live defines what life, success, and achievement are about for many of us. We are part of a much larger system, and we can make a difference within it.

While these seven areas were and are fundamental topics about enhancing the quality of life, in and of themselves, they weren't a call to action for the company. They never took off to generating the wider conversation we needed about sustainability throughout Fetzer. So those of us on the Leadership Team kept talking, and those discussions eventually led to E^3.

It was clear when we had hit on the right excitement-generator. Very soon after we rolled out E^3 it was part of every conversation we had about maximizing profits, saving energy, serving the community, or virtually any topic on the table. Once it took on a life of its own, we kept talking about E^3, pushing into new areas, reviewing how we acknowledged people for achieving goals in an E^3 format. The E^3 approach is now automatic and endemic. The conversation, you might say, is now having us.

It is vital in generating the conversation for you to be part of it personally as a leader. There is a lot of support, from all quarters, for talking about maximizing profits. Everyone in business reads business newspapers, magazines, and books aimed at furthering that dialogue. If you don't talk to your boss about profits for a week, it doesn't cross your mind that your boss might be thinking about something completely different. You know it's always top of mind.

It's different with a new conversation, and a new concept, especially one that doesn't have all that external support built in. Leaders need to start, nurture, and direct conversations about sustainability. We need to participate fully, creating space for others to express themselves fully. Practicing this consistently is essential. People do what they talk about, and if they don't hear their leaders talking about sustainability, they won't generate the ideas that are essential to sustainability success. If you don't talk, they don't care. We can't be everywhere at once, of course, so we also need to structure conversations about sustainability so they take place without us. Schedule regular get-togethers at various levels of the business, so people get used to talking about sustainability on a consistent basis. Another good technique is to mention sustainability in every gathering of any kind, no matter what the rest of the agenda is. Some companies use intra-company websites to keep certain topics in front of people on a daily basis, but in my view, no matter how vibrant the words and pictures are, a report about a conversation is not a conversation. When you reduce it to one-way communication on a screen, you drain most of the power right out of it. The reader is no longer a participant in that open, democratic process of exploration and discovery. It's a passive,as opposed to an active, involvement.

EXPANDING THE CONVERSATION

ONCE YOU GET THIS GOING in your own organization, no matter how big or small, your next role as a leader is to expand the conversation outside of it. Find people in your industry who want to talk about sustainability. They may be in Sweden and you talk via e-mail at first. It doesn't matter. The power of conversation will kick in and things will happen. You will be helping to shift the mindset of business from solely one of profits to one of sustainability. This is, ultimately, how we will change the world.

The conversation about sustainable business will grow so broad, deep, and influential that we will take it for granted. It will become an essential dimension of management, like understanding finance or manufacturing or brand development. We're a long way from that point now, but every individual who joins the conversation takes it another step farther. I invite you to join us, too.

FIFTH PRINCIPLE

YOU CAN'T PREDICT THE FUTURE, BUT YOU CAN CREATE IT

A few years ago I took my Leadership Team to a retreat in Monterey, California. Like most companies, we'd done our share of management training. Some worked, some didn't, but it was always my goal to vary the experiences so we would come away energized and refreshed.

The Monterey area is a mecca for golfers, and one of the events I planned for my team was a visit to a golf school run by Fred Shoemaker, who calls his method "Extraordinary Golf." The plan was to take a class, then play nine holes. My brother had given me Fred's book, and I knew that this legendary teacher saw golf as a metaphor for life. I allowed the team to believe we were just going to take a golf lesson, not a life lesson. I saw this retreat as an opportunity for our new team, with diverse backgrounds and interests and experiences, to gain insight into our business and build a closer relationship.

We went out to the practice tee and Fred had everyone hit a few irons while he videotaped us individually. Being taped in front of others can be unnerving, but we soon loosened up because Fred is a great teacher and he made it fun. I paid particular attention to my videotaped swings. I set myself up carefully, running through all the reminders golfers carry in their heads. Keep your head down. Eye on the ball. Elbows straight. Turn your hands over as you swing through the ball. The contact with the ball felt good, and I thought I had done pretty darn well.

Then Fred posed a new challenge for the team. This time he gave the first person an old club and pointed to a target a few dozen yards out on the fairway. He told her to set up as if she were going to take her normal swing, but to let go of the club and let it sail out toward the target. There would be no ball to hit. The thing she was supposed to hit was the target out on the fairway.

It took a while for this instruction to sink in, but one by one we did it. The clubs went flying every which way, and not always at the target. Fred kept videotaping each of us as we continued to throw clubs down the fairway. My club sailed out when I let go of it, and landed right near the target.

Then we gathered to watch the tapes of how we swung when we hit the golf ball and how we swung when we threw the club. I knew in advance that this exercise was coming, because it was described in Fred's book. I was sure that my swings would look pretty much the same. As the tape began to roll, I sat there stunned. My golf swing was so ugly, I could hardly look at it. It was the kind of swing I hate to watch in others: herky-jerky, too slow at some points, too fast at others, and my elbows, wrists, and hips all seemed to be the in wrong place at critical moments in the swing. I was more than embarrassed. I was crushed.

Then Fred cued up my club-throwing swing, and once again I was amazed. This time my swing was smooth, with a natural motion that had my whole body moving in perfect timing. It was hard to believe that the same person had executed these two totally different swings.

At that point, Fred the golf pro became Fred the philosopher. When we focus on the ball, he explained, our minds organize our body to hit the ball. When we focus on the target, our minds organize our body to hit the target. The point of golf, Fred reminded us, was not to hit the ball. It was to put the ball in the cup. By focusing on the ball, we were focusing on short-term results. We were seeing golf as 80 or 90 or even 100 little short-term events (depending on our handicap) instead of one big picture.

I have always been a very results-oriented person, and now I saw why my swing was so ugly when I focused on the ball. Hitting it was the first thing I could do that would have a result. So that's what my body organized itself to do. The most important result in my mind—and therefore for my body—was the first result I could get. This orientation made it more important to strike the ball cleanly than to let my body organize itself for the bigger purpose of hitting the target.

But when I changed my orientation to something much further out, my body created the necessary swing—all by itself. I could not bear down and get a short-term result. I could only open up and let fly toward the real target. That is the genius in Fred's method. If people focus on the target rather than the ball, their golf swing just naturally falls into place. It's in service of something bigger and farther away. The swing is no longer the problem to be corrected. It becomes the solution to the real problem.

My mind immediately went to where I spend most of my time in the business world. What I realized is that most companies are managing to hit the ball, but not always toward the target. Their orientation is toward what's right in front of them—a monthly or quarterly profit goal—and not to the real target further out.

This experience changed the way I looked at strategic planning. We all do strategic planning in business, and we would be remiss if we didn't. But I think we have all been concentrating on hitting the ball rather than the target. We're planning as if we could predict the future in increments: doing the same thing as last year, but at higher volume or higher quality or higher prices.

When I used to sit through planning meetings as the winemaker at Fetzer, my feeling was always that every new plan meant I had to buckle down and work even harder. I had to come up with some way to do more with the resources I had, and once I did that the plan would change again and I would have to do even more. When I became president, I had those same feelings, but with a lot more anxiety. Each step looked like a huge hurdle. How would we sell those next 100,000 cases? How would we penetrate that new market? How would we get product into Wal-Mart? How would I make that 15 percent growth number? No matter how well we did, the same challenges were in front of me the next quarter or the next year. It was hard to feel that we were getting anywhere.

Even worse, as we grew, was the sinking feeling that something outside our control could happen to derail our progress. A vine pest could wipe out a prized vineyard. A late frost could affect the yields our growers promised us. Bad corks could spoil the best wine we ever made. Competitive brands could erode our market share. We were trying to predict the future in the face of the future's inherent unpredictability.

ORIENTING AND ORGANIZING

FRED'S GOLF LESSON showed me that if Fetzer Vineyards had the right orientation to the target, we would naturally organize the process for achieving it. Once I realized that, I began to think about the future differently. My real targets were making a difference with my business and changing the world, not reducing this quarter's kilowatt hours or increasing this month's graduates from ESL classes. Those are important things and they need to be achieved. Even though the ball is not the target, you still need a ball to play the game. But the target's out in the future, and I wanted the target to naturally organize our process of reaching it, just like in Fred's golf swing exercise.

Then it dawned on me. The last thing I did on the tee before I threw the club was to look at the target and imagine my club hitting it. What if I stopped thinking of the future as this unpredictable thing (like where my ball is going to land) and imagined that I was already hitting the target? What if stopped trying to predict the future and just created it from already being there?

After working with this idea, experience tells me that it is another principle for sustainable leadership: *You can't predict the future, but you can create it.*

UNPREDICTABILITY AS AN ALLY

WITH THIS PRINCIPLE, we can make the future's inherent unpredictability become a positive, not a negative. We just have to create the future from the future instead of predicting it from the present. Then the processes for achieving it will organize themselves accordingly.

If I stand in the future and look back at Fetzer after we have become a six-million-case winery, I see things about today's four-million-case winery I can't easily see from the present. I can see all the areas where we're not behaving like a six-million-case winery. I can see people who are going to have to step up, and what kind of opportunities they're going to need along the way. I can see structural issues about production, efficiency, and distribution. I can see a marketplace that needs millions of new wine-drinkers.

Now my whole thought process about my business is different. What I listen for changes. What I observe changes. The conversations I have change. My perspective is now six million cases looking backward, not four million cases looking 10 percent ahead. My attitude also changes. Now I'm not in charge of coping with whatever future happens to me, I'm in charge of creating the future I want. The target is clear, my role is clear, and the business begins to move almost by itself.

The future begins to move, too.

In particular, unpredictability becomes my ally, not my enemy. Unexpected things that happen now fit a pattern I can more easily recognize. I'm not looking at them from the present and thinking that unexpected things are not supposed to happen. Instead I'm thinking that all kinds of things I can't foresee are going to have to happen for my business to reach the target. I *need* the future to be unpredictable. I *need* the unexpected. I'm actually helping to create unexpected events by stepping into the future and managing my business from there.

PAINTING A VIVID PICTURE

CREATING THE FUTURE from the future is a major way that we leaders earn our right to lead in a sustainable business. We are, after all, making the future our business. We're looking forward more than our counterparts in business ever had to, because now there are much bigger pitfalls out ahead of us as a society: global warming, melting ice caps, crop devastation, epidemics of disease, vast regions of social and political unrest (some of them equipped with nuclear weapons).

Actually creating a future that minimizes those pitfalls is part of our job as leaders.

Creating the future from the future is also one of our most important vehicles for getting out ahead of our newly empowered organizations, with their context, their passion, their freedom to discover and live what they know inside a much larger system. To lead this kind of organization, we leaders must shift from a perspective of incremental change to a perspective of transformation. We must stand in the future and look back at the way we came, instead of always standing in the present and hoping the future will look just like today, only bigger. The key is to paint a vivid picture of it. You need this not only for yourself to see, but also to make the future come to life for others in your organization. The point of the picture is not to accommodate the present, it's to accelerate the arrival of a particular version of the future.

Let me give you an example, from just ten years ago, so we can look back at how things happened not just in our imagination, but for real.

It was 1994, and there were some intriguing ideas teasing at my awareness. One was the "French Paradox," which is that people in France eat a higher-fat diet than Americans but have lower incidence of heart disease. After CBS aired a segment about this on *60 Minutes*, subsequent research confirmed one of the hypotheses for the paradox: drinking a moderate amount of red wine lowers the risk of heart disease. At the time, most Americans were drinking a lot more white wine than red, in part because many California red wines were rather challenging to the average consumer palate. We've gotten much better at making wines such as Cabernet Sauvignon and Zinfandel in a style that anyone can drink, but back then people who wanted to drink American red wine didn't have that many easy options.

Their best option, it occurred to me, was Merlot. Merlot is a smooth, easy-drinking red wine with a lot of fruit flavor. It's also a grape that gets ripe with great reliability, so it is less susceptible to weather variations that affect other red grapes. We hadn't made a huge commitment to Merlot at that point, selling fewer than 10,000 cases of our Eagle Peak Merlot the year before. On the other hand, no one else was staking their future on Merlot either. Much of the Merlot grown in California was blended into Cabernet Sauvignon, so few people drank it on its own. But if we could persuade growers to sell us their Merlot, we could bottle it and sell it to a populace that was becoming much more interested in the healthy qualities of red wine.

What would it look like, I wondered in 1994, if Fetzer put all these clues together first, and created a big new market for Merlot? So I created a vivid picture of 1999. In that future year, here's what the picture showed:

Fetzer Vineyards

1999 Vision for Merlot
written in 1994

We sell more than half a million cases of Merlot.

We are the number one selling Merlot in the country.

We are the number one selling Merlot in the top twenty markets nationwide.

When people buy a bottle of Merlot in a store or at a restaurant, the odds are that they are buying Fetzer.

I loved this, and shared it with my management team. They didn't love it, at least not at first. Instead they responded with objections: We didn't have existing contracts for anywhere near that much Merlot fruit, and we didn't even know if we could get people to plant more of it for us. We didn't know what kind of barrels we would need, or how we would pay for them. We didn't have space in the winery to produce another half a million cases of anything, much less something new. We didn't have our distributors on board to move that kind of volume. We didn't have Brown-Forman on board. We didn't know if people would even want to *drink* that much Merlot.

Of course, these were all the challenges they could see at that point, back in 1994. They were looking at the ball down at their feet, not out at the cup where we had an opportunity for a hole in one. I had to make the picture more vivid, so my team could join me in the future and look back at the path they had taken to get there. The pivotal moment came at our annual sales meeting in August of 1994. Everyone on the Leadership Team was there, including our head of winemaking, Dennis Martin. This was our favorite time of year. All the sales people came in from the road to join us at the winery, it was just weeks before crush, and the energy was pulsating.

I began painting my vivid picture of 1999, when we would have achieved our dominant position in Merlot. I described how we had achieved it with huge increases in grape purchases, big new plantings of Merlot, and total buy-in by our distributors. Then I had Dennis stand up. Everyone loves Dennis and he's been a big part of our success over the years. They cheered and applauded. As the noise died down, I said to the sales team, "In five years, you guys won't be able to sell as much Merlot as Dennis and his team can make."

You could have heard a pin drop.

In that moment, their picture changed. They were an enthusiastic group, always ready for new challenges and big goals. But as I had been talking, they had been seeing only what was going to come out of the chute at them: more cases of Merlot. Now they were seeing the whole winemaking enterprise committed to a much bigger target: creating a vastly larger market and dominating it. It was a different picture, a very vivid picture, and now they could see it. And I was telling them they were not pulling their weight. Within a few moments, they were getting their voices back. "Oh, yeah?" they said. "Only half a million cases? We get five whole years? Try us!"

That year we doubled our sales of Merlot, to 40,000 cases. Then next year we sold more than 125,000, and the year after that we passed 250,000 cases. In 1997, Eagle Peak Merlot was the top Merlot in the United States, generating more sales than any other brand. In 1998, we blew past my original target of half a million cases, and we were at or near the top in the 20 largest markets nationwide. By then the competition was fierce, with hundreds of Merlots flooding into the market from everywhere and at every price point. But we had been standing in that future years ahead of everyone else. In 2002, Fetzer was still making America's top-selling Merlot under $10.

The Merlot experiment galvanized people so quickly that I began to wonder if there was an even bigger picture out there for me to paint, one that would expand beyond how many cases of wine we produced and which markets we dominated. It would be a picture of sustainable success that included all those things, along with environmental and social successes that we could create.

One day I sat down and started writing out a vivid picture for the whole company, as a leader in sustainable business. (You can read it beginning on page 191.) This was back in 1994, when the year 2005 was more than a decade in the future. The very first paragraph offers a perfect example of the principle that you can't predict the future, but you can create it: "Fetzer will be recognized as the leading company in the world for its sustainable business practices." At the time I had never imagined this book—I could not have predicted it at all. Yet my vivid picture of the future led inevitably to the decision to write it. From the perspective of 2005 I'll look back at the book as a step toward Fetzer becoming more recognized for its progress as a sustainable business.

In the description crafted in 1994, I also included some examples of how our future would play out with regard to the environment, the community, and the world. Here are some of the things I envisioned, and what has happened since.

"An environment of learning that allows everyone to be able to speak English, thereby creating equal opportunity for growth and development." People at Fetzer tend to work long hours, and many of our production workers have families and second jobs that also place demands on their time. So when we began creating the future we saw an ESL (English as a Second Language) program that took place on-site during the workday. We sponsored the instructors, classroom, materials, and computers for ESL classes, and let employees from the bottling lines take ESL classes on paid time. It soon became apparent that our approach was motivating people to leave work for a paid break rather than to study English seriously, so we changed our policy: Employees got half-pay for the hour they were in class. As more students passed through the classes, the motivation level increased to the point that we didn't need even that incentive. Employees still pay nothing for the classes and materials, but now they take them on their own unpaid lunch hour. Our cellar workers and vineyard workers have also joined the ESL program, despite the logistics of bringing them to and from the winery during the day.

The local community college now grants credit to students who complete classes, which is a point of pride for people with teenagers.

Their own formal education may not include a high school diploma, but they've got college credits their kids don't have. Some of the classes now take field trips to local stores on weekends, to practice their English in a practical setting, and people who complete enough basic courses at Fetzer can flow right into more advanced classes at the community college. When we have E^3 meetings and read out the names of people who have completed an ESL class, there are dozens of people on the list. In my picture for 2005, I foresaw our Mexican workers speaking English when they attended parent-teacher conferences, made major purchases of cars and houses, and took trips around California with their bilingual kids. We're just about there now.

"By 2005, I can envision all our service and support vehicles operating with solar-powered electric or natural gas engines." I learned from this part of our vivid picture that technology moves and shifts in truly unpredictable ways, so the next time I step into the future of energy and transportation, I'll allow for even more flexibility. At this point, nearly all our service and support vehicles (for maintenance, housekeeping, facilities, and construction) are electric vehicles powered by our green-power supplier. Our forklifts are now powered through green power, too. Our large production and delivery vehicles, including our vineyard tractors and our 18-wheelers for moving barrels and case goods, use bio-diesel fuel in varying percentages. Bio-diesel works just like petroleum-based diesel fuel, but it comes from renewable plant material. In still other vehicle categories, we're trading down for smaller, more fuel-efficient carts, trucks, and autos. We're experimenting with hybrid-fuel vehicles and other options, and as fast as we can find the E^3 balance that justifies them, we'll adopt them. When fuel cell vehicles arrive, we'll be among the first to have them.

"I can see where Valley Oaks will be recognized as a leader in creating food and wine concepts within the sustainable approach to living." I've already described the organic garden at our Valley Oaks Food & Wine Center. I should fill in the rest of this actual picture. We now have a large, airy culinary theater with seating for 60 people, adjacent to a small lake, at one end of the garden. We use the theater for classes of all kinds, not just cooking. Valley Oaks also has a thirteen-room bed and breakfast so we can host visitors, students, instructors, and visiting chefs 365 days a year. Our tasting room at Valley Oaks has a popular retail store and a cafe, patronized by winery visitors and locals alike. So just in terms of the physical plant and capabilities, Valley Oaks is unique as far as the wine industry goes.

The slate of events and classes is also a standout. The Brown-Forman Global Wine Education program teaches wine history and technology, organic farming techniques, and trends to our industry partners each year, and we've also launched a program with the University of California at Davis to teach sustainable winegrowing practices that will be available to every winegrower in the state. Cooking classes occur throughout the year, with nationally known chefs such as Julia Child, Emeril Legasse, Mark Miller, and Bradley Ogden. Our own executive chef, John Ash, teaches not only at Valley Oaks but all over the country, often using recipes from his book, *From the Earth to the Table* (Dutton, 1995). In 2003, Valley Oaks' reputation went international when it placed the first winery garden ever into the prestigious Chelsea Flower Show in England.

These are just three examples of how the vision we had for 2005 created results from the future. There are many more aspects we are still exploring, and of course before 2005 even rolls around we'll be painting a bold new picture of Fetzer for everyone at the company to step into.

Now I'd like to offer a vivid picture that's far broader than the future of Fetzer as a sustainable business—one of a sustainable world.

In this sustainable world, business leaders are accountable to shareholders not just for financial returns, but also for social and environmental returns—because shareholders insist on all three and because business leaders will deliver them. Everyone is part of the same larger system, and sees a need to start healing it. More people, in more companies, feel deep pride in their business. They are living what they know both at home and at work, in their community and in their company. There is no internal division that makes them doubt or question their purpose, because there is no need to check their values at the door when they get to work.

In this future, no one goes hungry. No one lacks shelter. No one lacks medical care. On an Earth of so much natural abundance, and in a species capable of producing so much wealth, we should be amazed that such conditions exist at all. In a world where business steps up to lead the way toward sustainability, we'll be amazed at how quickly they disappear.

Manufacturing processes and consumption patterns begin to evolve rapidly in symbiotic ways toward the elimination of waste in any form. We need fewer and fewer resources per unit of production, and continually create less waste per unit of consumption. All the hallmarks of successful business—innovation, efficiency, continuous process improvement, supply chain management, you name it—are applied to making economic activity more sustainable. "Waste" comes to seem just that: wasteful. Eventually, every child knows what nature has always known: everything is part of the larger system, and must be fully used up in order for things to remain in balance.

As a result, there is clean water in every corner of the earth. Carbon emissions are falling relative to economic output, not rising.

Synthetic chemicals are rare, absolutely necessary exceptions to the norm of organic agriculture. Endangered species are escaping extinction and reversing their long declines. Rainforests are expanding, and deserts are shrinking. The earth, too, reverses its course and begins to regenerate itself faster than we can deplete its resources.

In this future, the sources of human suffering—disease, war, economic distress—become targets of successful businesses. Leaders closest to these issues create conversations with everyone else in business to explore and discover how to solve them, prevent them, and remove them from the political game board. Business leaders are unafraid to speak out about unsustainable political opportunism, because they know they speak for millions of shareholders and employees. They know they speak for the earth. They know that a sustainable world is one that works for everybody.

In this future, religious tolerance is spread through business success, because sustainable businesses find larger, unifying purposes that bring people together across political and cultural frontiers. Economic well-being spreads more equitably. Fear and hatred are increasingly isolated by a rising sense that humanity is joining together to save itself from self-destruction. Respect for the human spirit becomes part of global self-awareness, making human rights abuses harder for people to imagine, much less commit.

This picture may sound idealistic, but I believe we can create it. Being able to conceive it, and make it vivid for ourselves, is fundamental. That's the whole point of this chapter. But we can't keep pushing the picture out into the future and leave it there as something we imagine. We have to start doing things today that make the idea of sustainability a reality. There is a way to make an idea's time come, and we need to start putting it into practice.

SIXTH PRINCIPLE

THERE IS A WAY TO MAKE AN IDEA'S TIME COME

Let's step into the future and create a vivid picture of your organization. It could be a team of three or a corporation of 300,000. Regardless of the size, you and they share a purpose that provides a vibrant context for the work you're doing. Everyone sees how the organization fits into the larger picture, not just within the business or the industry you're in, but within the economy, the society, the world. Everyone understands that they can make a difference with this organization. In this aligned state, turf issues rarely arise, and when they do, everyone sees the higher purpose that resolves them. Teamwork comes naturally because everyone is aligned on the picture. And their leader, is able to step out into the future, look back, and create new possibilities for them as individuals and as an organization.

As a result, people are transcending their job descriptions and becoming the source of ideas, not just a resource for executing them. Their vision of the future motivates them to bring aspects of themselves to work that they used to leave home: values, passion, creativity, commitment. The various conversations you have—with individuals, with groups, with people outside the organization—always have the same touchstone, which is your purpose, and the same aim, which is creating the future from the future. People are always asking what's possible, and when someone answers a question by saying "I don't know," people understand that those words are not the end of the conversation, they're the beginning of exploration and discovery. New ideas are emerging, and they're getting bigger all the time.

Now the question becomes: How do you make these new ideas' time come? What step can you take in behalf of those ideas that will affect both the present moment and all future possibilities, for your organization as well the larger system?

You can take a stand.

Taking a stand is something most business leaders already know how to do within the context of maximizing profits. Mergers, acquisitions, and spin-offs often arise from management committing itself to a new business model. The absence of these actions can also represent a strong stand, as it did when Lou Gerstner declared that he would not break up IBM when he took over in 1993. It's the same with big commitments in the area of research and development. When Intel sold off its memory chip business years ago, it was taking a stand for the higher margins the company could earn in logic chips. When Genentech's founders launched the company more than twenty-five years ago, they were taking a stand for a new way of creating pharmaceutical medicines. When Herb Kelleher founded Southwest Airlines, he was taking a stand on affordable air travel. In all these cases, the companies involved have become prosperous standards for their industries in terms of both operational and financial performance.

I'm suggesting that companies can create a sustainable future in the same way, by taking stands on environmental and social issues.

DuPont, Nike, and Xerox are among the growing number of companies that have taken stands on zero waste. Patagonia took a stand that it would use only organically grown cotton in its popular sportswear line. Robert Redford's company, Sundance, took a stand on environmentally responsible ski resort development. Amazon.com, Hewlett-Packard, Coca-Cola, and other companies took a stand that they would expense stock options, no matter what regulators or lawmakers decided. These decisions are not incremental. They are not about doing the same thing as last year, just a little bigger. They are either/or, do/not-do decisions, the kind that don't just reflect change. They create change.

ADAPTING THE WORLD TO YOUR WORD

THIS IS THE DIFFERENCE between an idea whose time has come, and an idea whose time we must make come. People are always looking for the idea whose time has just arrived, so they can be part of it. They talk as if they are doing something futuristic, but they're really going with a trend in the present. They're looking at what is already happening, and saying, yeah, we want to get in on this, too. No matter how right or cool or profitable it may be to go with that trend, they are simply adapting their word to the world.

A stand is about doing the opposite: it's about adapting the world to your word. A stand creates the trend that others want to follow. When you commit yourself to something that doesn't currently exist, you create real change, not incremental change. You can't actually see how you're going to get there, and the world is probably telling you that there's no way you *can* get there. But now people are at least talking about your stand, and how it could be achieved, and what it would mean. They're starting to live in the future you see and deal with it from their own perspective. No matter what else happens, you have already had an effect.

When Mahatma Gandhi led his famous Salt March in India in April of 1930, Britain maintained a monopoly on making and selling salt—an essential element of the human diet. Gandhi took a stand that the monopoly would end, and he told the people of India that the monopoly would end. He told them they would end it by producing their own salt from seawater. The British promised to arrest anyone who tried it. Gandhi didn't care to adapt his word to that world. He was adapting the world to his word. He set out from his home with fewer than 100 supporters, and walked nearly 240 miles to a beach on the Indian Ocean. During the time it took him to walk that far, the people of India began to realize that Gandhi was serious. He was going to the beach to collect salt, despite the British monopoly. By the time he got to the beach, the British were ready with a large force to block him from reaching the sea. What they didn't expect was that a much larger group of Indians had joined Gandhi during the last 50 miles. Gandhi's stand was working faster than anyone expected. He was adapting the world to his word with every step he took.

While the British used batons to beat back and arrest the unarmed and nonviolent Indians, Gandhi and his followers simply kept coming. Finally the jails were full, the British were exhausted, and the Indians kept coming. Reporters for the world's newspapers and magazines also came. Their reports of nonviolent Indians being beaten by British soldiers simply because they wanted salt from their own seashore was a turning point in Britain's occupation of India. The monopoly ended because Gandhi took a stand on it. Soon Britain left India entirely.

TAKE A STAND, NOT A POSITION

TAKING A STAND is different from taking a position. Gandhi did not take a position that the British salt laws were bad, or unfair, or illegal. They may have been all that, but he was not interested in taking a position about them. He wanted to end them. So he took a stand. There is a huge difference.

People take positions relative to things, and if the things shift, the positions do, too. Politicians are always talking about their positions. They write "position papers," they debate their positions, and then they change their positions depending on what other politicians do. Positions are the essence of partisan politics, and one of the things that cause legislative logjams. People are for their party position, not a larger purpose. No alignment can take place, because the positions are all relative to each other.

I think it surprised many people when the U.S. Congress voted to grant President George W. Bush authority to invade Iraq late in 2002. Many people opposed that resolution, and they were loudly vocal about it. But once Bush took a stand that he was going to change the regime in Baghdad no matter what, and once he set that context for people in a clear and inescapable way, the Congress dropped its partisan positions for a larger purpose of changing the regime in Iraq.

The distinction between stands and positions is important for sustainability, because positions can subtly undermine sustainable leadership. Positions keep us in a state of reaction rather than initiation. We're just dancing with our closest competitor, or our critics, trying to hold some position relative to them. Stands, on the other hand, are not relative to anything. They don't change based on the politics of the day or if someone objects. A stand actually includes all the objections and positions everyone else might take about it. It includes all the various points of view people might have, their considerations, and their particular circumstances.

The stand does not adapt to these things. It includes them in its larger purpose, just as a hole on a golf course includes the tee, green, cup, fairway, rough, and all the possible shots that have ever been hit and could ever be hit on the hole. The hole stands for a particular way of challenging golfers, and it doesn't change because different golfers show up or because of what they think about the hole. Once that hole is laid out, we all play it as best we can. We adapt to it, not the other way around.

A stand for sustainability must be big enough to have the same effect: The world adapts to the stand, not the other way around. The stand includes every way it could possibly be approached by people, every way it could possibly be fulfilled, every possible outcome of its fulfillment. It's big, it's unwavering, and it's enduring. The whole world might shift around it, the stars might align differently, and all kinds of unexpected things might arise to bring about its intended result. And the stand is still there, unchanged, still including everything.

DIMENSIONS OF A STAND

EARLIER, IN CHAPTER 4, I talked about the letter I wrote to the wine industry, in which I suggested that our industry take the lead in eliminating chemicals from our farming. This suggestion brought up concern from the industry leaders who responded. They pointed out that the wine industry doesn't use as many chemicals as other agricultural specialties. This is a position many people have unthinkingly taken in the wine industry. You can tell it's a position because it's a stance relative to something else. In absolute terms, the chemicals are still going into the ground and water, but as long as other people use even more chemicals, this position says, the wine industry isn't responsible for the larger problem.

When you take a stand, you don't care where anyone else is on an issue, and how much impact you're likely to have. You do it because you can, because you have to, because the world is crying out for it. You take the stand because you believe it will make a difference.

There are several important dimensions of taking a stand that leaders need to understand, because once you take a stand as an organization, things will start to shift.

First, a stand is personal for each of us. It's about seeing a personal possibility of making a contribution and fully expressing our commitment to that. When I think about our stand on organic viticulture, it connects me to my immediate, personal desire to make a difference, right here, right now, in behalf of the earth. The more people who take a stand personally, the more powerful it will be.

Second, each of us is responsible for its completion. We don't have a part in the play, we *are* the play. Everyone is the source of the stand, not just a resource to it. Each of us is responsible for finding new opportunities, new solutions, new ways forward.

Third, each of us is responsible for generating the conversation about the stand. This grows naturally out of the first two dimensions. You're responsible for making the stand come alive for others, to attract them to it as a possibility, and to advance its discovery and exploration.

Fourth, each of us is responsible for remaining open to whatever happens. There are obstacles out there you can't anticipate, and opportunities you don't expect. With a stand, you have a firm intention—and then you must be alert to however it might play out. You keep the conversation going to further the cause, no matter how surprising it might be. All the objections and roadblocks may look like problems, yet they should be expected and viewed as opportunities to recommit to the stand, discover an unexplored path, and spur you to unconventional solutions.

LANDING A MAN ON THE MOON

IN MAY OF 1961, President John F. Kennedy stood before a joint session of Congress and took a stand: "... this nation should commit itself to achieving the goal, before this decade is out, of landing a man on the moon and returning him safely to the earth. No single space project in this period will be more impressive to mankind, or more important for the long-range exploration of space; and none will be so difficult or expensive to accomplish."

Earlier in this same speech Kennedy proposed a number of positions on disarmament, civil defense, and the economy. But it was different when it came to space. He could have taken a position that the United States would be a leader in space technology, and that we would devote a certain amount of resources to that end. If he had said that America was simply going to outdo whatever the Soviet Union did, it would have put the Soviet Union in charge of the space conversation. It would have been good enough to see what they were doing and do a little better than that. We would have made progress, but without the sense of urgency that calls us to ask of ourselves something we never asked before. The sense of purpose that brings forth greatness would have been missing.

A stand elevates us above all our considerations, all our points of view, and organizes us in service of achieving a new possibility. Kennedy's stand meant it didn't matter what other countries did. It didn't matter what the economy did. It didn't matter how big a rocket we would need, or what a moon landing would look like. All those things were included in his stand, along with all the ways you could fulfill it, all the obstacles you might hit, all the conversations about it, all the objections people might have to it. It was absolute, it was going to happen, and all the aspects of it could then unfold. This is a vital lesson for leaders. It is essential to include in your stand that its fulfillment is not only possible, it's inevitable.

Of course, in May of 1961, none of the Apollo rockets or moon landers had been built. They didn't exist. But two things more important did exist: Kennedy's stand, and the context of possibility that he set for it. His stand already acknowledged that it would be hard and costly. But when he said no other project "will be so difficult or expensive to accomplish," he was taking the accomplishment as a given. The issue was not whether we would or could do it. The issues were how much it would cost and how much we would have to invent to get a man to the moon and back before 1970. Those issues were placed inside a larger context, which was achieving a new possibility. The stand made it inevitable that we would actually achieve that new possibility.

MY STAND

TAKING A STAND contains all the same elements as building a sustainable business. You have to set a context in both cases, which the Kennedy example illustrates. You also have to generate conversations about the stand, and structure them to cover all the territory on a consistent basis. You have to see your people as capable of participating in the stand and fulfilling it and create the space for them to express themselves fully. And painting a really vivid picture of the future enables people to experience the power of the stand.

In 2002, I began painting a vivid new picture for Fetzer, in which all the vineyards we own, manage, or contract with would be farmed organically. We are already the California winery with the highest number of certified organically farmed acres under ownership and management. This was the case even after we spun off our Bonterra brand in 1995 and it became a separate company within Brown-Forman. We could have repeated the Bonterra process and created another "organically grown" product under the Fetzer label, but by 2002 our internal conversations had evolved past that point. Our own vineyards were organically farmed, but provided only about 20 percent of the grapes we needed. I was now imagining virtually all of our fruit being organically grown, which would involve our contract grape farmers in a bold new adventure. In my vivid picture, we would achieve this milestone by the end of the decade.

When 25 of our managers from across the company came together to have a conversation about this picture, their reactions ranged broadly from enthusiasm and excitement to upset and anxiety. Our field representatives were immediately concerned that our existing community of growers might not accept it, or be able to convert their vineyards fast enough. If they didn't convert, they would lose our business. How could we make sure they made the transition successfully?

Our winemakers were concerned about how they would

make the transition from using mostly conventional grapes to mostly or all organic grapes. Would we blend all the grapes together in the transitional seasons, regardless of how they were farmed, and just keep making the same wine we were making now? Or would we start bottling certain wines that came only from organically grown grapes, and steadily increase the percentage of such new bottlings while we phased out the older, conventional wines?

All these issues came up, and more. To many questions about how we would do things, my answer was the same: "I don't know." It wasn't that the people in that meeting thought our goal was impossible to achieve. Most of them had already seen things occur at Fetzer that they never imagined were possible. They already had a culture of doing new and different things in order to achieve a broader purpose. So even as they listed all their concerns, they were doing it in the context that we would overcome them somehow.

Once everyone had raised their issues, we were able to organize them by topic or area of the company—in other words, we were able to structure the conversations we needed to have. One would involve our growers and their agricultural supply companies, to educate people about alternatives to synthetic toxic chemicals used for weed control. One conversation would involve all the financial issues, including farming costs and what we would pay for the grapes. Another concerned winemaking and all the interim logistics of handling both organic and conventionally farmed grapes, from harvest through to the final blend in the bottle. Yet another revolved around all the branding, sales, and marketing issues.

GOING PUBLIC

FINALLY WE ARRIVED at a point where we had everyone talking and people were starting to see the vivid picture of the future more clearly. Now it was time to take a stand: to go out in public, in the eyes of the world, and announce what we wanted to do. Of all the reasons to take a stand, this is one of the most important. By going public, I was showing the world not only the future I saw, but also my conviction that we could create it despite the potential obstacles. That is a big way that a stand makes an idea's time come.

By taking this stand in public, I see us changing the world, right now. My vision includes multimillion-case wineries using only organic fruit, and huge tracts of vineyard land farmed in harmony with the earth and the surrounding community. It may take others a while to wrap their minds around this idea,but they can't deny that some of us see it already, are working toward it, and believe it will happen. The industry now has a new possibility, and the efforts of Wine Institute and California Association of Winegrape Growers within a single year show how quickly a new possibility can move from off-the-wall to down-the-middle.

Finally, if people have ideas or interests related to a new possibility, taking a stand on it gives them a focal point for expressing them. This last point is vital, because I believe everyone has ideas and interests related to a more sustainable world. Everyone wants a healthy Earth, a strong community, and economic prosperity. There may be other things we disagree on as human beings, and our level of awareness about sustainability may differ sharply, but at this point in the history of our species, billions of people have the same fundamental goals and desires and can see that others share them.

Going public with a stand for sustainability taps into this huge potential for concerted action, and that's what gets results in the end. I see this already in our stand about organic farming. Everyone at Fetzer is giving up chemically farmed grapes, not just the growers and our vineyard people. Everyone is helping create a company that's built that way. Everyone is helping change the larger system so that the company can succeed that way. And when we succeed, everyone is going to share in the results and the rewards. This time it's for the whole industry. This time it's for the world and everyone living in it. This time it's for the earth.

YOU ARE ALREADY ON THE PATH

THIS APPROACH MAY SEEM idealistic to some. I believe that creating a sustainable world is not only realistic, it's the inevitable outcome if business takes a clearer look at the larger system, understands the opportunities, and moves toward sustainability with all the imagination, leadership, and organization that successful businesses bring to bear every day. By business I mean business leaders, those individuals who are already in a position to marshal resources, motivate people, and orient an organization toward a new target.

These qualities of leadership need never change. But your role as a leader will begin to shift. You will look inside yourself, and you will find things you care about. That's where it all starts. You will notice what you feel strongly about and start to bring those things into your conversations and your interactions with others. You will notice that those interactions themselves can reflect your most deeply held values. You'll find yourself rethinking the context of your whole company, and realizing that with the right context, your job can become much more about creating the environment in which others will fulfill the destiny you see for the world. It can become much more about seeing what's ahead, stepping into the future, and creating the future from that perspective.

We leaders and the principles we manage by are a product of the past. Those principles got us to where we are today, and in many ways it's a great place to be. Free markets are helping to create free countries. Human liberty is helping to strengthen human rights. We can communicate with each other as never before, we can sell our products and services in more places and more ways than ever, and we can forge much stronger bonds with our customers, suppliers, and shareholders.

From here, the best way to respect the past is to be responsible for the future. If there is anything you love about the world that created you, that you grew up in, and that you became successful in, then it's time to find a way to sustain it far into the future.

Leaders like you see a new possibility for business. You are changing your thinking, your perceptions, and your conversations because of what you see. You are letting the fixed definitions that may have formed your role as a leader soften, so that you can accept a new kind of leadership role. In all these ways, and others too, you are already on the way forward. You are already bringing about a change that people everywhere are ready for, a change that the earth will embrace, because it will result in a sustainable world that works for everyone.

In the end, there is one simple truth: We are where we put

our energy, our efforts, and our attention. This is how we show up in the world as individuals, and it's the same for our businesses. The decision is ours.

AFTERWORD

GRAPES INTO WINE

Premium wine grapes have been cultivated and refined for thousands of years. Many of the most popular wines come from grape varieties originally developed in Europe. The rugged, geologically complex terrain of Mendocino County offers many varieties a good home, because there is an extremely wide range of soil types and microclimates. Some grapes do best on hillsides, some better in flat spots; some want more water than others, some want more rocky soil. We have all those conditions in Mendocino County, in varying combinations. Winegrowers can spend their entire careers adjusting which grape varieties and rootstocks are planted in which spots in their vineyards, to get the maximum quality and yield in each location.

Grapes are planted in the vineyards using different systems of spacing, trellising, and irrigation, depending at what the grower is aiming for. The land can be planted and farmed to yield as much as 10 tons of grapes to the acre, or as little as a single ton. We generally keep our yields in the low end of the range, around 5 to 6 tons per acre.

In late fall, after the grapes are harvested, the vines lose their leaves and go dormant for the winter. During this time, winegrowers prune each vine back to just a few buds. These new buds pop out in March, followed in late spring or early summer by flowering and pollination. By May, miniature bunches of tiny green grapes appear. They rapidly expand in size, taking up moisture through the vine's roots and storing sugars created by photosynthesis in the vine's leaves.

In August, white wine grapes such as Chardonnay and Sauvignon Blanc turn yellow and gold. Cabernet Sauvignon, Merlot, Zinfandel, and other red grapes turn crimson, purple, dark blue, or even black. In late August or early September, winemakers walk the vineyards, seeking the moment when the grapes contain the right levels of sugar and acid—skins carry flavor and sugar which ferments into alcohol, while acids confer structure and balance.

When the grapes reach the desired point within this range, they are harvested. At our winery in Hopland, we process 30,000 tons of grapes each harvest. Crush, as we call the harvest, usually lasts from around the first of September through the end of October.

FERMENTING WHITE WINE

BOTH RED AND WHITE GRAPES go through a crusher/destemmer machine that removes the grapes from their stems and crushes the fruit to produce the "must": a thick soup of juice, skins, and seeds. From this point the fermentation process is different for red and white wines.

White wine is made by fermenting only the juice of the grapes, without the skins and seeds. So after the must comes out of the crusher, we send it directly to the wine press to extract the juice from the skins and seeds. The press is a large metal cylinder, lined with stainless steel mesh and containing an inflatable bag. The must is put into the press and the bag is inflated, which presses the skins against the mesh allowing the juice to be collected at the bottom of the press. The juice is then sent into a settling tank in the winery. We collect the skins and seeds from the press and compost them for vineyard fertilizer. The white grape juice in the tank is refrigerated and allowed to settle, usually for 24 hours, until the temperature is about 45°F, and any solids from the skins and seeds that may still be in the juice have gotten to the bottom. The clean juice then goes to a fermentation tank and yeast is added. Yeasts consume the sugars in the wine, converting them to alcohol and carbon dioxide. Yeasts are naturally found on grape skins, and sometimes are present in high enough concentrations in vineyards to start the wine fermenting soon after it's pressed. We generally add cultured yeast that imparts the qualities we're aiming for in the finished wine.

At our winery, we have 100 white wine fermentation tanks ranging in size from 1,000 to 18,000 gallons in capacity. We can control their temperature, which lets us speed up or slow down the fermentation (yeasts are more or less active at different temperatures). We generally keep the temperature down, between 50°F and 60°F, so that the yeasts work at a slow, even pace over two to six weeks. This lets the flavor and character of the grapes develop fully before all the sugar is turned into alcohol. If we did not take this time, we would miss many of the nuances and subtleties that make white wine such a pleasure. When all the sugar is gone, the wine is called "dry." Some white wines are made by stopping the fermentation press before all the sugar is utilized, and those types are called "sweet." Once they have no more sugar to eat, the yeasts expire and settle out of the wine to the bottom of the tank. The wine then moves to a blending tank, where it is combined with other wines to make a finished blend for bottling.

MAKING RED WINE

THE PROCESS FOR RED WINE FERMENTATION differs from the white wine process in one major regard: the grape skins and seeds are left in the tank while it ferments. This is done for two reasons. Most important, the skins and seeds contain important chemical elements, including an acid called tannin, that give red wine its aroma, flavor, texture, structure, and ability to age. Without these elements, the wine would appear very much like white wine. It is also critical for the juice to ferment with the skins in order to extract the color, because red wine juice itself is clear.

When the red must (the skins, seeds, and juice) comes out of the crusher/destemmer, it is sent immediately into a red wine fermentation tank. We then add yeast and let the fermentation start. A red wine tank is almost the same as a white one, except it has an extra door at the bottom so the skins and seeds can be removed after fermentation. At our winery we have 65 red fermentation tanks, ranging from 1,200 gallons to 16,000 gallons capacity.

Red wine ferments at a higher temperature than white wine, from 80°F to 95°F. We let the temperature rise with red wine because this encourages the grape skins to give up their color and flavor compounds to the liquid. Because the temperature is higher, the process finishes much faster, usually in seven to 10 days. The carbon dioxide produced by the yeast pushes all the skins to the top of the juice, where it forms a crust called the "cap." To get the best flavor and color from the skins, this cap has to be broken up several times a day and mixed back into the juice. Wineries use different methods for this. Some pump juice from the bottom of the tank over the top of the cap to break it up, and others push the cap down into the juice.

Most red wines are fermented dry, to the point that there is virtually no sugar left. When fermentation is complete, the cap is allowed to float to the top, and the wine is pumped from the bottom to a storage tank. We remove the skins and seeds from fermentation tank, and press them once more to remove any remaining liquid. All the wine is then sent to oak barrels for aging. The skins and seeds go to compost.

Barrel aging does several things for the quality and taste of the wine. The tannins we extracted during the fermentation process can make young red wine taste harsh or bitter. Storing red wine in a barrel for a period of time, from nine months to two years depending on the wine, reduces the bitterness of the tannins, and makes the wine softer and easier to drink. Red wine is also improved with some air contact, and the barrel allows just enough air transferred through the oak staves to get to the wine. Barrels come in several shapes and sizes, but most hold between 60 and 70 gallons of wine.

After the wine has spent the right amount of time in the barrels, it's moved to a blending tank, where it can be combined with other wines before bottling.

We create both our red and white wines by blending in two ways. One type of blending involves more than one kind of grape. For example, we will often include a little Merlot in our Cabernet Sauvignon, to add some softness and aroma. We may do the same in reverse, adding a little Cabernet to a Merlot to give the wine backbone or structure. Our white wines such as Sauvignon Blanc, Riesling, and Gewürztraminer also may have a small percentage of another white grape blended in to achieve a certain style. These decisions are made after many, many trials, and the finished blend varies for every wine we make, every year. With some of our wines, the goal is to keep the final blend as consistent over time as possible, so consumers can count on a favorite wine to have a consistent style—one that they know goes with certain foods and gives them pleasure year after year. With other wines, especially our reserve reds, the goal is maximum vineyard expression, allowing for unique nuances each vintage.

The other type of blending is within each grape variety itself. Our Sundial Chardonnay, for example, comes from dozens of different vineyards in several growing regions. Each vineyard responds to each growing season differently, producing different flavors and aromas in varying intensities. So we blend different lots of Chardonnay from different vineyards, in different quantities, each year, to produce the final blend. We do this with all the wines in our larger blends, to make sure we're using the best lots of wine that make economic sense at each price point.

Once we've made the blend, the wines are filtered and bottled. White wines are generally distributed within one year after their harvest date, while reds, which benefit from additional time in the barrels, are usually released into the market within one or two years.

GROWING WINE GRAPES ORGANICALLY

ORGANIC FARMING is an important stage in restoring agriculture to its natural roots. It's not the only way to farm in harmony with nature, but it's a very effective one. It's also a method that can be certified, so consumers know with assurance that they're buying food or wine that was grown without chemical additives. Fetzer farms 2,000 acres that are certified organic, and we're working with our independent growers to try to convert their 9,000 acres to organic farming by 2010.

Organic farming focuses on the life of the soil. Soil develops its own richness by providing a home for plants, insects, and microorganisms that feed each other, fertilize each other, and renew each other. If you put healthy soil under a microscope, you see that it's literally crawling with life. The living things add all kinds of substances to the soil, including oxygen, water, minerals, and decomposing plants and insects. The microorganisms and subsurface inhabitants, such as earthworms, break up the soil and reduce the organic matter into nutrients that are then taken up by the plants on the surface, starting the whole cycle again.

Conventionally farmed soil contains a lot less microscopic life and a lot more evidence of chemicals. Some chemicals target living things that could harm or compete with the crops, and others artificially feed the crop plants that have to live in poisoned soil. Over time, this cycle leeches the life out of the soil. Organic farming achieves the same goals as conventional agriculture—feeding the crop while controlling potential disease and damage—without departing from nature's own cycles and mechanisms.

To feed the soil, organic farmers create and apply natural compost. At Fetzer, we use the skins, seeds, and stems left over from our winemaking each year, and mix it with cow manure. This mixture sits for a year, while microbes start working their magic to break down the organic material in it. By the time we spread the compost over the soil, it is both a rich food for the vines and a powerful preventative against disease in the vineyard.

To manage insects that could inflict damage on their crops, organic farmers attract other insects that prey on the vine's predators. Ladybugs and lacewings are examples of such beneficial insects. They eat the mites that can seriously harm a grapevine. To attract good bugs we plant the flowers, legumes, and other plants that they live in naturally. We call these "cover crops" and grow them between the vine rows. Once the cover crop dies back, we cultivate it into the soil as "green manure."

Organic farming takes patience. It requires that a grower spend more time in the vineyards, evaluating the soil and the vines and the cover crop. There are no quick fixes, such as spraying toxic chemicals to wipe out a dust mite invasion, or spreading some chemical fertilizer to make the leaves greener for photosynthesis.

At Fetzer, we are looking beyond the 2,000 acres of vineyards we own and considering the land outside and beyond their borders. These areas contain another level of diversity of insects, plants, and animals that can contribute to the health of the vineyard. Gophers and moles, jackrabbits and deer, and a whole range of insects can invade a vineyard from outside its bounds. That makes us think of their natural predators as our allies. Owls feed on gophers and moles, bats and bluebirds consume large quantities of insects, and bobcats and mountain lions prey on jackrabbits and deer. Within the vineyards, we have introduced chickens and sheep. The sheep graze on grasses in the dormant season, which keeps the grasses in check and turns it into manure. The chickens will eat all sorts of insects. They're particularly good at eliminating cutworms, which can cause severe damage to the first new buds on the vines in early spring. Chickens also scratch up the soil, opening it up for more air and water and organic matter to penetrate the surface. Forty chickens per acre work better than a rototiller, and they're much better company for our vineyard crews.

Still further out on the natural farming spectrum is biodynamism, a philosophy of farming developed by Rudolph Steiner in Europe in the 1920s. It includes organic farming practices, along with additional methods aimed at helping growers work even more closely with natural processes, seasonal cycles, and planetary rhythms. Most wine drinkers have never heard of biodynamic farming, but some premiere producers in France have quietly been farming this way for years, and winemakers everywhere else are slowly discovering that those they most respect are, in fact, far ahead of the rest of the industry in their farming practices. Now there are biodynamic wineries in California, Oregon, and Washington.

FETZER HISTORY
AND
FUTURE DEVELOPMENT

A FETZER VINEYARDS TIME LINE

1955 Barney and Kathleen Fetzer move to Ukiah from Oregon, seeking a rural setting to raise their growing family. Barney works as a lumber broker and Kathleen manages a family of 11 children through the years.

1958 The Fetzers purchase a 720-acre run-down ranch in nearby Redwood Valley. Barney and his oldest sons John and Jim begin to revitalize the property and plant an 80-acre vineyard. John Fetzer begins to convert a former sheep barn into a winery.

1968 The Fetzers produce their first commercial vintage: 2,500 cases of red table wine.

1976 Sales reach 50,000 cases per year, enabling Barney Fetzer to retire from the lumber industry and focus on the winery.

1977 Paul Dolan is hired as winemaker. Dolan, whose extended family includes three generations of winemakers, has recently completed studies at Fresno State.

1980 Fetzer Vineyards produces its first collection of vineyard-designated Zinfandels, from Ricetti, Sharfenberger, and Lolonis Vineyards.

1981 Fetzer Vineyards purchases the 1,130-acre Sundial Ranch, located 25 miles south of Redwood Valley. Production reaches 200,000 cases. Barney Fetzer dies unexpectedly.

1982 Fetzer Vineyards launches Sundial Chardonnay and the Bel Arbors brand.

1983 Fetzer Vineyards launches its Barrel Select brand.

1984 Production reaches 540,000 cases. The Fetzer family purchases Valley Oaks Ranch, located one mile east of Hopland. Along with new vineyards, the property's barns, houses, and outbuildings will become a food and wine center for entertaining and educating the wine trade.

1985 Dennis Martin is hired as assistant winemaker. Twenty-one acres of pear orchards at Valley Oaks are removed to create the Dooley Chardonnay vineyards. Organic gardener Michael Maltas is retained to design a five-acre organic garden, to include over 1000 varieties of fruits, vegetables, herbs, and flowers—both edible and decorative. Work on the garden begins in summer 1986. Construction of the Food & Wine Pavilion, a state-of-the-art culinary classroom, also commences.

1986 Eighteen additional acres of Chardonnay are planted at Dooley vineyards. Twenty-nine acres of Chardonnay are planted at the Blue Heron vineyard, along the Russian River. Sales reach one million cases.

1988 Valley Oaks Food & Wine Center opens on Highway 101 at Highway 175 in Hopland. Construction begins on a new winemaking facility near Hopland. Fetzer Vineyards is named "Winery of the Year" in its industry category by *Wine & Spirits* magazine (the first of nine such awards in the next 12 years).

1989 Organic grape growing begins. Fetzer Vineyards is named "Winery of the Year" in its industry category by *Wine & Spirits*.

1990 Famed wine country chef John Ash is named Culinary Director for Fetzer Vineyards, and culinary courses are offered at Valley Oaks Food & Wine Center. Visiting celebrity chefs include Julia Child. Fetzer Vineyards is named "Winery of the Year" in its industry category by *Wine & Spirits*.

1991 Fetzer Vineyards launches Bonterra wines, produced from 100 percent organically grown grapes. Initial introduction includes red table wine and Chardonnay. Fetzer wins first of several California Waste Reduction Awards Program (WRAP) awards for outstanding efforts in energy and resource conservation. Fetzer Vineyards is named "Winery of the Year" in its industry category by *Wine & Spirits*. Paul Dolan is named "Winemaker of the Year" by Dan Berger, writing in the *Los Angeles Times*.

1992 Brown-Forman Corporation purchases Fetzer Vineyards. Paul Dolan is named president, Dennis Martin is named winemaker. Consolidation of all winemaking into the Hopland facility begins. Production reaches 2.2 million cases. Fetzer Vineyards is named "Winery of the Year" in its industry category by *Wine & Spirits.*

1993 Ground is broken for the Mendocino Cooperage, making Fetzer Vineyards the only winery in America with on-site barrel-making capabilities. Fetzer revamps the labels and packaging for its entire product line. Fetzer Vineyards is named "Winery of the Year" in its industry category by *Wine & Spirits.*

1994 Fetzer Vineyards is named "Winery of the Year" in its industry category by *Wine & Spirits.*

1995 Ground is broken for a new administration building, production and warehouse facilities in Hopland. Fetzer spins off its Bonterra family of organically grown wines into a separate company.

1996 The Fetzer Vineyards tasting room is relocated to Valley Oaks Ranch, and the ranch is renamed "Fetzer Tasting Room & Visitor Center." A second tasting room opens in the coastal village of Mendocino. *From the Earth to the Table: John Ash's Wine Country Cuisine* by John Ash with Sid Goldstein is named "Cookbook of the Year" by Julia Child and "Best American Cookbook" by the International Association of Culinary Professionals (IACP).

1997 Fetzer is named one of the 10 best waste-reducing companies in the state by the California Department of Conservation.

1998 Fetzer Vineyards wins the most medals for wine at the California State Fair. A new Reserve Collection is introduced. Fetzer Vineyards is named "Winery of the Year" in its industry category by *Wine & Spirits.*

1999 Fetzer winemaking operations are completely consolidated in Hopland. Ground is broken on a new winemaking facility located in Paso Robles. Fetzer wins the inaugural "Award for Environmental Excellence" from *Business Ethics* magazine and "Climate Wise" Partnership Award from U.S. Environmental Protection Agency. Fetzer earns ISO 9001 certification, an internationally developed, prestigious standard for business process quality. Fetzer Vineyards is named "Winery of the Year" in its industry category by *Wine & Spirits*.

2000 The new winemaking facility in Paso Robles is brought on line. Fetzer releases the first bottling of Valley Oaks Syrah.

2001 California State Assemblywoman Patricia Wiggins presents Fetzer Vineyards with a "Wine Community Good Citizenship Award." Fetzer Vineyards is named an Official Supporter of the 2000, 2002, and 2004 U.S. Olympic Teams and the 2002 Olympic and Paralympic Games.

2002 Paul Dolan celebrates 25 years at Fetzer Vineyards. Five Rivers Ranch wines from Paso Robles debut in six U.S. markets. Fetzer Vineyards launches two new brands, Prato Verde and Five Hills Blue, that use only organically grown grapes.

FETZER ENVIRONMENTAL RECORD

Sustainable organic agriculture

Fetzer Vineyards is the largest grower of certified organically grown grapes on the North Coast and one of the largest in the world. One hundred percent of its 2,000 farmed acres are certified organic through California Certified Organic Farmers (CCOF). The organic vineyards are farmed without the use of pesticides, herbicides, or chemical fertilizers.

Product design and use of recycled materials

Bottles are made from 40 percent recycled glass (post-consumer waste) and case partitions are made from 100 percent post-consumer chipboard. New flange-top bottles, introduced on most Fetzer premium varietal wines, eliminate the need for capsules altogether.

Waste reduction/elimination

Through a company-wide waste reduction effort and the recycling of all bottles, cardboard, plastic, aluminum, paper, antifreeze, waste oil, fluorescent tubes, and glass, Fetzer has reduced waste to landfill by 94 percent since 1990.

Water quality/water treatment

In 1998, Fetzer and UC Davis created a natural filtration system employing gravel filters and a planted reed bed, reducing the need for traditional "aeration" ponds. The treated water is used on the winery's organically farmed grapes.

Supplier environmental management

Fetzer was the first winery in the United States to buy corks direct from the source in Portugal and ship them in large containers, thereby eliminating packaging. The corks are processed and de-dusted at the winery, imprinted with the brand name, and lightly coated with paraffin/silicone.

Green architecture and energy efficiency

The winery finished construction in April 1996 of a new 10,000 square foot administration building in Hopland. It is one of the world's first large-scale uses of rammed-earth construction and features recycled doors and timber. Photovoltaic panels were added to the building in June 1999 and supply 75 percent of the building's electricity.

Support of the green community

Fetzer supports a wide range of organic and farming-oriented organizations, including the Organic Farming Research Foundation and the California Certified Organic Farmers. The company is also a sponsor of the Business for Social Responsibility Annual Conference, the Eco-Farm Conference, and the Bioneers Conference.

Chlorine-free winery

In 1998, the use of chlorine was eliminated in favor of alternative methods of sanitation.

Stewards of the land

Fetzer has undertaken numerous projects to enhance the environment. It worked with the Audubon Society to provide a sanctuary for blue herons and habitat for birds of prey. Working with U.S. Fish and Wildlife Service, the company restored and enhanced tributaries of the Russian River. Employees also regularly participate in The Russian River Cleanup.

Carbon emission mitigation

In March 2000, the effects of GHG (greenhouse gas) were assessed, with the help of Natural Logic, Inc. With the switch to 100 percent renewable power, electricity-generated GHG effects were reduced to zero, and with reductions to landfill, solid waste emissions have been reduced 92 percent. Using bio-diesel (vegetable oil) in farm equipment and to provide commuter vans for employees reduces consumption of fossil fuel.

Being green is good business

Fetzer initiated a new business program in 1998 to create a triple bottom line: along with economic considerations, impact of any business decision upon the employees and the environment is fully evaluated.

Awards

Business Ethics magazine awarded Fetzer its "**Award for Environmental Excellence**" (1999).

The US Environmental Protection Agency presented Fetzer with its **"Climate Wise" Partnership Award** (1999).

The EPA awarded Fetzer with its **"Green Power Leadership" Award** (2001).

The EPA awarded Fetzer the **"Stratospheric Ozone Protection" Award** recognizing the company's exemplary efforts and achievements in protecting stratospheric ozone (2002).

California Integrated Waste Management Board selected Fetzer for the **Waste Reduction Award Program (WRAP)** for the ninth year (2002).

THE FUTURE OF FETZER: A VISION OF 2005

Internal memo written in 1994 by Paul Dolan

Our vision for Fetzer is that by the year 2005, Fetzer will be recognized as the leading company in the world for its sustainable business practices. By sustainable business practices, I would see that all business decisions and actions would be socially just, environmentally sound, and economically viable.

This would mean that everyone in the company would have a clear picture of where the company was going and how the company wanted to be represented in the world to the consumer. If all employees had a clear picture of what the company wanted to be like in the year 2005, they would be able to make independent decisions that make a contribution to our company goal. They would take into consideration their community and their neighbors, whether they be fellow employees, suppliers, distributors, or members of the human race. They would also consider how their decisions affected the environment, whether their decisions contributed to the health of the planet, reduced the planet's resources, or contributed to maintaining diversity, and they'd have a basic understanding of reducing, reusing, and recycling.

Each employee would also have the responsibility of making sound economic decisions, decisions that supported the health and growth of their company.

This is a huge undertaking, which is going to require first of all a clear sense of direction by the company leadership, and support and coaching from all levels of management.

The possibility here is to create a distinct and powerful company that has a purpose far greater than that of simply huge profits. The possibility is that our business can be a leader in the world and act as an example for other companies to aspire to.

The opportunity here is to provide a rewarding and fun lifestyle for our people and to share that with other businesses throughout the world. The basic concept here is that our human nature is to want to give and contribute to others. If we can design a company that supports that human need, we will make a difference in the world and ultimately be very profitable when we accomplish this; we will have achieved the ultimate success a company could ever hope for.

The opportunity here is to create a holistic way of looking at our business and leave no stone unturned in the arenas we choose to participate in.

Human Environment

Within the human environment, I think we can provide not only education for our employees but also education for our children. We can provide a day care center that gives our children a healthy, active learning environment that will be supportive of family values, community needs, and joyful living.

I envision a fun, simple country design that allows kids to be able to work in gardens, take hikes, learn from nature, and have an appreciation for the simple life.

I see an opportunity to create an environment of learning for all of us such that change is welcome, an environment of learning that opens our minds to looking at life as full of possibility.

An environment of learning where the IQ of the team far outweighs any one individual.

An environment of learning that supports us in continuously recreating ourselves as new challenges and opportunities arise.

An environment of learning that supports us in being responsible for ourselves and others we are in contact with, i.e., family, friends, and other members of Fetzer.

An environment of learning that looks at life from the place of "I don't know," rather than, "done it, seen it, and been there."

An environment of learning that allows everyone to be able to speak English, thereby creating equal opportunity for growth and development.

An environment of learning that provides employees the opportunity to reach out to their community to look for opportunities to do volunteer and support work.

An environment of learning that creates relationships with suppliers and distributors such that those partnerships propel both organizations well beyond each organization's individual goals.

An environment of learning where employees feel safe with the concept of learning, where they are not concerned about being judged or evaluated or concerned with failure.

An environment of learning where learning begins with dialogue in which members suspend assumptions and think together to solve problems or chart the future.

An environment of learning in which Fetzer can be a leading business in its educational programs for children in the area of agriculture. I can see where Valley Oaks will be a world-recognized learning center for kids and the wonderment of agriculture.

Physical Environment

By the year 2005, I can see us using half the current power, even with the growth that we will experience. We can do this by expanding our knowledge on construction methods, i.e., insulation, building materials, technological advances. We can do this through commitment to looking for new ways to produce our products, innovative systems designs, and reaching out to suppliers for support. I believe we can integrate new solar technology to reduce our dependency on electricity and liquid fuels.

By the year 2005, I can see a recycling center constructed by 100 percent recycled materials that will house used materials for future construction and maintenance projects, an automated recycling center supporting us in our goal of recycling 100 percent of our waste.

By 2005, I can envision all our service and support vehicles operating with solar-powered electric or natural gas engines.

In 2000, I can see our packaging being produced from 100 percent recycled materials, utilizing nontoxic inks and glues. I can see us no longer using capsules, thereby reducing waste, using smaller labels and recycled glass. I picture this packaging as being state-of-the-art in its design.

By 2000, I can see where Fetzer will reduce its employees' use of liquid fuels for their vehicles through company provided transportation. This will not only save on fossil fuel but also support a sense of family and community within Fetzer.

By 2000, I can see Fetzer being toxic-chemical-free in all aspects of our business, from cleaning supplies in the winery to restroom cleaning agents, to fossil fuel use, safe glues, etc. I can see where we will not only reduce our water usage by half of our current usage of water gallons per wine gallon produced, but in addition create regenerative waste water ponds supported by solar power.

I can see where our construction in the future will consider the types of materials used and their impact on the depletion of the planet's natural resources, how the construction improves the quality of our people's lives, and how our construction supports the natural environment.

Economic Environment

I can see where Fetzer Vineyards will be the most profitable winery in the industry based on the standards of return on the investment.

I can envision where Fetzer Vineyards will be considered the leader in supporting its employees with benefits and pay.

I can see where Fetzer Vineyards will be able to support community outreach programs, artistic programs, and community development programs. I can see where Fetzer can contribute 10 percent of its gross to these programs.

Valley Oaks (Food & Wine Center)

I can see where Valley Oaks will be a source of inspiration for consumers such that they can see how great their lives can be when it is structured around respect for the land.

I can see where Valley Oaks will be an example for sustainable living.

By the year 2000, I can see where Valley Oaks will be growing and producing 100 percent of all the food it serves.

I can see by the year 2000 where Valley Oaks will be recognized as a leading educational center on sustainable living through such practices as permaculture, seed saving, biological diversity.

I can see where Valley Oaks will provide the awareness and the respect for food for the gift and pleasure that food provides.

I can see where Valley Oaks will be an example of how a company can be sustainable, which will be represented by organic farming, permaculture, solar power, electric vehicles, bicycles, recycling, water conservation, community outreach programs.

I can see where Valley Oaks will be recognized as a leader in nutritional awareness, healthy diet, center-of-the-plate design, respect for agriculture, and respect for the fact that a healthy soil produces healthy plants, produces healthy people.

I can see where Valley Oaks will be recognized as a leader in creating food and wine concepts within the sustainable approach to living.

I can see where Valley Oaks will be considered the leader in program designs for kids' education and experimental learning through our commitment to the community.

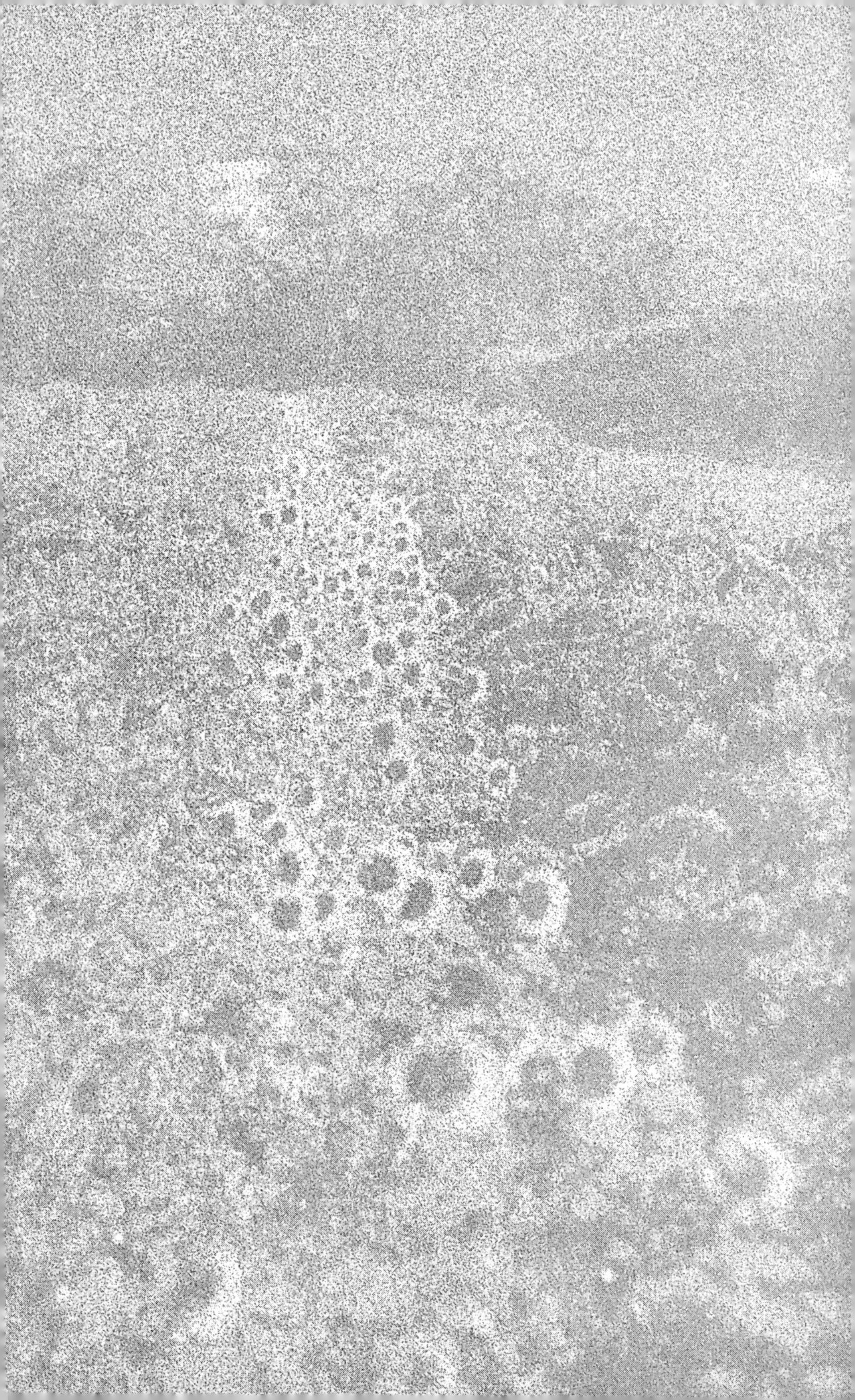

RESOURCES

It would take a great many pages to list all the resources available to people interested in sustainability. Here we focus on books, organizations, and websites that informed and inspired us in writing this book—and which can be springboards to further research and initiatives of your own.

BOOKS

PAUL HAWKEN HAS BEEN an influential voice in the sustainability arena for more than a decade. In ***The Ecology of Commerce: A Declaration of Sustainability*** (HarperBusiness, 1993; $23.00), Hawken looked at how businesses can operate more like nature does: producing and consuming in balance rather than imbalance, so that they do not destroy the world around them. This book remains a powerful introduction to thinking about your business in a whole new way, with illustrative examples that bring the metaphor down to practical reality. More recently, Hawken's ***Natural Capitalism: Creating the Next Industrial Revolution*** (Back Bay Books, 2000; $26.95) shows how some exemplary companies are practicing "a new type of industrialism" that is more efficient and profitable even as it helps preserve the environment. This book simultaneously creates a sense of urgency for action now and a sense of hope for the future.

Lester R. Brown is another author with multiple books on sustainability and related topics. His latest is ***Plan B: Rescuing a Planet Under Stress and a Civilization in Trouble*** (Earth Policy Institute, 2003; $28.00), which focuses on population and climate issues. Of more general interest for business leaders is ***Eco-Economy: Building an Economy for the Earth*** (Earth Policy Institute, 2001; $16.00), in which Brown describes the role business could play in altering the economy to preserve the environment for all living things.

More than 10 years ago, business consultant John Elkington wrote ***Cannibals With Forks: The Triple Bottom Line of 21st Century Business*** (New Society Publishers, 1998, $15.00). His latest book, coauthored with Bob Willard and Oliver Dudok van Heel, is ***The Sustainability Advantage: Seven Business Case Benefits of a Triple Bottom Line*** (New Society Publishers, 2002; $26.95). If you need dollars and cents to justify movement toward sustainable business, look for them here.

A number of CEOs of successful businesses have produced books that describe their own process for progressing toward sustainability. We recommend ***The Soul of a Business: Managing for Profit and the Common Good by Tom Chappell*** (Bantam Books, 1993; $21.95). Chappell is CEO of Tom's of Maine, and in his book he discusses how mind and spirit can work together to help a business compete for profit and market share. His story also shows that a business can be a formidable competitor and still express its commitment to the environment, its employees, and its broader community.

For a more philosophical approach to sustainability, explore ***The New Business of Business: Sharing Responsibility for a Positive***

Global Future edited by Willis Harman and Maya Porter (Berrett-Koehler, 2000; $19.95). The world is changing at an accelerating rate—some would say an alarming rate—and the essays in this book argue that business must take an active role in guiding and shaping that change. In other words, business must make the future its business. Some of today's most creative thinkers in the area of business and global change contributed to this anthology, making it a stimulating source of new ideas and insights.

To learn more about the people most likely to become early adopters of sustainability on a societal level, look into ***The Cultural Creatives: How 50 Million People Are Changing the World*** by Paul H. Ray (Three Rivers Press, 2001; $25.00). Ray identifies "cultural creatives" as a broad slice of society defined not by geography or income or religion, but by how people in that slice interact with their own culture. If you find that this definition works for you, it will help you understand why you see the world as you do—and that there are millions of people who see it much like you do.

Success in sustainable business will require that business leaders get the maximum possible contribution from everyone in their organizations. One of the first books that looked at leadership from this perspective was ***Servant Leadership: A Journey into the Nature of Legitimate Power and Greatness*** by Robert K. Greenleaf (Paulist Press, 1991; $14.95). This book makes the case that leadership is not so much a privilege as a responsibility: A leader's primary role is to support his or her people to achieve their own greatness rather than to control them for personal glory.

Leaders of sustainable businesses must also get comfortable with constant change. ***In Leadership and the New Science: Learning About Organization from an Orderly Universe*** (Berrett-Koehler, 1992; $15.95), Margaret J. Wheatley shows that every organism in nature is in a constant state of nonequilibrium in order to encourage growth, development, and evolution. The message for business leaders is that change is both necessary and natural.

There are a great many business books devoted to the quest for excellence or success, and there will be many more. One that stands the test of time for us is ***Built to Last: Successful Habits of Visionary Companies*** by James C. Collins and Jerry I. Porras (HarperBusiness, 1994; $26.00). One of the book's important messages is that successful businesses identify and align themselves with a core purpose and use that purpose to inspire and motivate them to continually reach new heights.

For readers interested in a better understanding of sustainability in the wine business, we can recommend two recent books. In ***Real Wine: The Rediscovery of Natural Winemaking*** (Mitchell Beazley, 2000; $24.95), Patrick Matthews writes from a European, somewhat historical, perspective about a small but influential group of growers and winemakers who are taking a more sustainable approach to their business. Hilary Wright takes the consumer's point of view with ***The Great Organic Wine Guide*** (Judy Piatkus Publishers, Ltd, 2000; $22.50), in which she describes organic wine and winegrowing, what's available from different countries, and how to buy it for your own table.

ORGANIZATIONS AND WEBSITES

THERE IS A RAPIDLY GROWING NUMBER of organizations and websites promoting various aspects of sustainability, and it doesn't take long to find them online. Earth Policy Institute (**www.earth-policy.org**) is a good place to start. You can quickly educate yourself about sustainability issues, ranging from the challenges we face as a species to a road map for changing our shared future. Equally valuable is the ability to download a copy of ***Eco-Economy*** by Lester Brown. If you want to focus on the social responsibility inherent in managing a sustainable business, click over to Business for Social Responsibility (**www.bsr.org**), an organization dedicated to helping businesses succeed economically while respecting the earth, its people, and its future. Tools, training, and other resources are available to members and nonmembers alike. To learn how to eliminate waste from your business, start with the Zero Waste Alliance at **www.zerowaste.org**.

The "Ecological Footprint of Nations" created and updated by an organization called Redefining Progress (**www.redefiningprogress.org**) is a quick way to get a handle on the sustainability challenge facing human society. Another "dashboard" for determining the gravity of our situation is the "2002 Environmental Sustainability Index" created by the Global Leaders for Tomorrow Environment Task Force of the World Economic Forum. The Task Force's report is online at **http://www.ciesin.columbia.edu/indicators/ESI**. The United Nations is also a good source of data and trend analysis, gathered and presented by its Sustainable Development division (**www.un.org/esa/sustdev/**).

INDEX

ILLUSTRATIONS

ABOUT THE AUTHORS

PAUL DOLAN has been president of Fetzer Vineyards since 1992, having served previously as Fetzer's winemaker beginning in 1977. In addition, he is managing director for new products and strategic development with the wine group of Kentucky-based Brown-Forman Corporation, which owns Fetzer Vineyards. At Fetzer, Dolan's commitment to environmental stewardship and sustainable business practices, including organic farming and resource conservation, has been successfully integrated into day-to-day operations. His vision and management of the winery have resulted in numerous awards over the years in recognition of Fetzer's quality wine and environmental commitments. Dolan has been a past recipient of the prestigious "Winemaker of the Year" designation given by Dan Berger, wine columnist for the *Los Angeles Times.* A native Californian descended from three generations of distinguished winemakers, Dolan graduated from Santa Clara University with a degree in business and finance and holds a master's degree in enology from California State University, Fresno. He is on the board of directors of the Wine Institute and of Business for Social Responsibility and is founder of WineVision, a trade organization promoting wine in the United States.

THOM ELKJER is a career freelance writer based in northern California. His published work includes a novel, four books of non-fiction, dozens of feature articles in national magazines, and appearances in eight anthologies of international travel literature, as well as numerous book reviews, profiles, and other pieces for newspapers and magazines. As wine editor for *Wine Country Living,* he regularly reaches a national audience of high-net-worth households with his descriptions, commentary, and reviews of the world's wine and wine country. Elkjer's books include *Adventures in Wine: True Stories of Vineyards and Vintages* (Travelers Tales, 2002), *Escape to the Wine Country* (Fodor's, 2002), and *Savoring the Wine Country* (Harper Collins, 1995). He is a graduate of the University of California at Berkeley.